This is a gentle book emerg
would meet regularly and s]
valuable to them, knowing C
life and going on to live a cc
at the end of the journey they would meet their ____,
one who had been helping them all along. It is a book whose
chapters are most accessible, and though it is dealing with the
theme of pressing on – 'this one thing I do' – we see that it is
a shepherd's staff that is encouraging and delivering them, not
his rod striking their backs. I felt that I could follow the Lord
to the end when I had completed this book. Grace can keep me
going ... And you too.

Geoff Thomas
Conference Speaker and author, Aberystwyth, Wales

This book comes saturated with Scripture proofs and with a
profuse sprinkling of quotable quotes. It is a book about spiritual
progress in the Christian life, showing that Jesus intends for
His disciples to follow Him, and to continue well to the end
of life's journey here. This book challenges the reader; it will
convict; it will comfort and encourage. It will also warn about
becoming complacent. The author uses the Biblical accounts of
actual people, drawing lessons for us to improve our Christian
lifestyle. Not all those written about finish well, and the author
does not gloss over their 'blemishes'. Read this book, take up its
message, and commit yourself by grace, to pressing on. Your
Christian living here can only be enriched, and your confident
hope will be that you finish well.

Malcolm MacInnes
Retired Minister, Kingsview Christian Centre, Inverness

Pressing On, Finishing Well is for anyone who wants to take
the measure of their life, no matter their age. Through humor,
personal candor and biblical illustrations, Michael Black takes
readers on a journey to understand that the end of their lives is
determined by every minute leading up to that pivotal moment.
But I suspect that those of us who are caring for elderly parents
or looking at the finish line looming closer for ourselves will
find the greatest comfort and exhortation in this book. I highly

recommend it for taking stock of your current fruitfulness and purpose in your life, to re-orient yourself to entering the joy of your Master.

Carolyn McCulley
Author of *The Measure Of Success* and *Radical Womanhood*

The Christian life is pictured in Scripture as a race, and the key point of this metaphor is that we must run with the aim of finishing well. Sadly, many Christians start their race with zeal and enthusiasm but fail to sustain their momentum to the end. Drawing lessons from selected biblical characters, and with insightful practical applications for our everyday lives, Michael Black encourages us to strive to finish well. This is not just a book for older Christians, those nearing the end of the race, or those who sense they are flagging, but will inspire everyone who is running and wants to keep going. It challenges us to ensure that our love is rooted in Jesus, and to make our love for him our greatest treasure. It leaves us with a glorious vision of heaven that will motive us to press on and win the prize.

John Stevens
National Director, FIEC

LEARNING FROM SEVEN
BIBLICAL CHARACTERS

PRESSING ON
FINISHING WELL

MICHAEL BLACK

CHRISTIAN
FOCUS

Copyright © Michael Black 2019

paperback ISBN 978-1-5271-0337-5
epub ISBN 978-1-5271-0404-4
mobi ISBN 978-1-5271-0405-1

First published in 2019
by
Christian Focus Publications Ltd,
Geanies House, Fearn, Ross-shire,
IV20 1TW, Scotland
www.christianfocus.com

A CIP catalogue record for this book is available from the British Library.

Cover design by Kent Jensen

Printed and bound by
Bell & Bain, Glasgow

Contents

Dedication

Winers & Wives

To my original audience, my dear and steadfast friends. If I finish well, it is in no small measure because of your godly influence in my life. So Gordon and Jean, Glenn and Donna, Leo and Sue, Dave and Diane, Steve and Linda, John and Pam, Tommy and Jeanne, and Kevin and Terrie, thank you for listening to these messages year after year at our beach getaways. Even more, thanks for loving this old, sinning saint.

My Family

The Winers and Wives were the impetus for this book but my family is with whom I most want to share it. What husband doesn't want his wife to finish well? What father doesn't want his children to finish well? For all the advice I've given (good and bad), for all the examples I've set (good and bad), this book represents my life's message to them: 'We get back up for the glory of God.' Pegi, Eli, Kati, Jackie, Peter, and Mike, Anita, and Kaitlin, my prayer is that this would resound in your hearts when I am gone and become part of your life's message—and the grandtreasures after you.

Acknowledgements

A book is never about one person. It is a collaboration, sometimes intentional and professional, sometimes personal and informal. With that in mind, I would like to acknowledge three people in particular who have been influential in the publishing of this book.

This book made it to press because of Rosanna Burton of Christian Focus. She believed that a man who had never written a book before (me) had a message for people in the second half of life. Rosanna, who is not in the second half of life, understood my passion. I am most indebted to her.

Dr. Larry Dixon is a saint. He worked with a first-time author and endured that particular editing agony with grace and patience. Where this book reads well, credit Larry. I am still cringing at all the errors he found. And he is probably still twitching because of those same, numerous errors. Any remaining errors and failures in this book are mine alone.

Finally, Carolyn McCulley. Carolyn is an accomplished writer and speaker; and, most importantly, a woman of outstanding character. And she still referred me to Christian Focus. Thank you, Carolyn, for gracious and wise advice.

Gloria in Excelsis Deo.

Introduction

The worth and excellency of a soul is to be measured by the object of its love; he who loveth mean and sordid things doth thereby become base and vile; but a noble and well placed affection doth advance and improve the spirit unto a conformity with the perfections which it loves. (Henry Scougal)

HOW THIS BOOK CAME ABOUT

I have been blessed to know a particular group of men for many years. We met in the same church, although we are spread across different churches now. All are married with grown children. We come from a variety of professions—government and private sector managers, engineers, a writer/editor, a salesman, and a technology guy who can't tell us what he does or he would have to kill us. And all of us are committed Christians, having actively served in many contexts in our church: worship leader, home group leader, all of us servants. But what brought us together as concerns this book was … wine.

Years ago, one of the guys, Gordon, took an introductory class on wines of the world. He then invited us to make wine with him. Four of us took him up on the offer. Shoot, of course we did! We were going to make real wine! After buying our wine kits, we met every couple of weeks in Gordon's basement to perform the next wine-making task. It's a several months' long effort. Each time we completed a particular wine-making task, we would sit down in Gordon's kitchen and drink wine that we had bought since the wine we were making was still in process. We'd bring cheeses and other food to eat. And we talked. About everything. Families, the church, ourselves, theology, politics. We argued. Debated. Explained. Listened. Encouraged. We asked hard questions that we had kept to ourselves. Personal questions. Because we trusted each other, we talked openly and freely, without fear of being silenced or shamed. What we talked about stayed with us. We talked about our doubts and concerns and questions without fear of being corrected as sinful or characterized as gossipers. We invariably discussed things in light of our Christian faith and understanding of the Bible and how it might apply to whatever we discussed. We loved each other through it all. And we drank wine as we did. They were some of the richest times of biblical fellowship I have ever experienced.

Our wine-making was relatively successful (although we hadn't planned on producing thirty bottles of wine per kit!). But we discovered that we loved the fellowship more than the fermentation. Eventually, we stopped making wine but we continued to get together. Still do after more than ten years. Our little group quickly grew from 4 to 10. We called ourselves the Winers and yes, we intended the double entendre. We drank wine. And we 'whined'—that is, we talked and asked questions. To be clear: we didn't get drunk. We didn't gossip. We shared our lives over wine and food and fellowship. We critiqued and questioned our lives and each other, our church and the world. We worked hard to think the best about everyone. We became even better friends. And I would like to think that we became better Christians.

Then Gordon, bless his heart, had another great idea. He suggested we go to the beach with our wives over a long weekend and eat and drink wine. So we did. We went to Bethany Beach, Delaware, where we stayed in a large beach house. We loved it. We went in the late fall, so it wasn't very crowded. We talked. We played games. We walked on the beach. We made dinner together. We drank wine. We rested. We ate. We recharged. We drank more wine. Because it was the weekend, we decided to have a Sunday service with the twenty of us. We worshipped to a guitar. And I was invited to share a message. We've been doing that for ten years now (although we lost one dear couple to Minnesota a few years back).

Those messages at the beach are the source material for this book. I chose a theme that has long been on my heart: finishing life well. Each year since then, the message has been tied to that theme. Those messages are the foundation of this book. It is written as if I were sharing this with you at the beach on a Sunday morning—talking about something that will happen to all of us.

THE END IS NEAR

Someday soon, I will be dead. I don't know when but whether by accident, disease, or simply old age, I shall breathe my last and pass through the veil. My friends and family will no longer see me. I will no longer walk on the earth. I will be gone. Everything on this earth will come to an end for me.

- I won't be able to kiss my wife.

- I won't be able to watch my children and grandchildren grow older.

- I won't be able to take those trips I had hoped to

take.

- I won't visit with my friends.

- I won't be able to lose that weight or exercise like I wanted.

- I won't be able to follow through on any of those resolutions I made.

- All of my wealth will be of no value to me. It will go to others.

- And most of what I own will be thrown away.

The story will be finished. The last page will be turned. The book will be closed.

The unspoken but undeniable truth is: I will begin to be forgotten by this world as soon as I die. Actually, I've realized that this forgetting begins before we die. As we move, take new jobs, retire, we are forgotten. Think of throwing a stone in a lake when the waters are calm. You are the stone. The lake might be work or church or where you once lived. You make a splash. But that time we spend at work or at church begins to fade away like ripples on a lake as soon as we leave. And those fading ripples accelerate once we die. Let me give you an example: I don't remember much about my grandfather and know nothing about my great-grandfather. And I am family. Who else is alive who remembers them? Further back than them? Silence. The same is going to happen to me.

My impending death doesn't depress me or scare me (too much). I am in my 60s and I have been thinking about death on a regular basis for much of my adult life. Not in some dark, morbid fascination with death and dying but in a thoughtful, contemplative way. I find that facing the prospect of death from time to time helps me live my life differently and, hopefully, better.

Furthermore, I am simply more and more aware that, soon, the story of my life will be complete. My father died of a heart attack at eighty-four. As I write this, I am sixty-three. According to *Health, United States With Chartbook on Long Term Trends in Health* (put out by the Center for Disease Control and Prevention), at age sixty-five, I, as a white male, have eighteen more years to live. Barring some unexpected catastrophe that means time is getting short. Eighteen years just doesn't seem all that long when you are in your early 60s. My inevitable death looks far closer now than it did in my 20s or 30s or 40s.

THE OVERARCHING QUESTION

Here is the overarching question that I have asked and thought about all these years: Will I finish well? Will the story of my life end on the upward trajectory I hope for or will it end ingloriously?

I ask this question, mindful of choices I've made in the past and choices I am making now. There are lots of regrets about my past. Lots. The story of my autobiography would be, 'Don't Do It This Way!' But I also am aware that the choices I am making now play into how I finish. It's not over yet. All of it leads to the question, how will I finish?

I've run three and a half Marine Corps Marathons. Once in my 30s. Once in my 40s. Once in my 50s. Suffice it to say, my times were not boast-worthy. But finishing those races was. You finish the marathon at the Iwo Jima Memorial. There is a large crowd at the end, cheering every finisher. It is a slight uphill run at the very end of 26.2 miles. (Really? Uphill? Only the Marines …) Each time I finished, I tried to run as hard as I could. I am pretty sure that to the spectators watching me, I was barely trotting. But I gave it my all. As exhausted as I was, it was crossing that finish line that mattered. Was there a temptation to quit earlier on? Yes. Did I hit the wall earlier on? Yes. Those and other challenges were there during the race but I crossed the line. And at the end of the race, a Marine greets you. He or she wraps you in a foil blanket, bends down and unties your timing chip from your shoe. He or she then hangs a medal with a red, white and blue ribbon around you. The Marine then congratulates you on finishing, whether you are first or last. 'Congratulations, sir.' It is a moment to remember. Finishing life is like running those marathons. Do I press on to finish well or do I quit? Do I give in? What keeps me going? And what do I hear at the end?

What about you? Pretty soon, you will be dead too. Maybe not tomorrow. Maybe not in 10 or 20 years. But the end of your story is coming and probably sooner than you want.

How will your story end? Will you finish well or badly? And what will you hear?

WHAT THIS BOOK IS NOT ABOUT

I recall reading somewhere that in the 1800s everyone talked about death but no one talked about sex, while in the 1900s everyone talked about sex but not about death. It's an oversimplification, of course, but it has its merits as a commentary on Western society.

That seems to be changing in the twenty-first century, perhaps due in part to the Boomer generation's need to talk incessantly about whatever phase of life they are going through and now they are starting to die in numbers. Hence, we now have a fairly substantial deposit of literature on death, from assisted suicide, to estate planning, to how to postpone death by all types of schemes and means, from diet to exercise to gene therapy. And there are plenty of books and articles on living in our end years: how to eat and travel and even how to have sex.

This book is not about that.

For all the books out there on death and dying and our final years, there do not seem to be many books about tracing the arc of your life as you approach death with increasing speed and asking, 'How am I doing?' Or, rather, 'How do I gauge the life I've lived, especially the end game?' Or, 'What questions should I be asking about whether or not I will finish well?'

That is what this book is about.

WHAT DOES IT MEAN TO FINISH WELL?

A reasonable question with many possible answers. Many people would say that finishing well is having substantial savings that allow you to live comfortably, even prosperously. Perhaps it means living out your life with the glow of accomplishments and the respect of your profession and friends. Perhaps it is finding new meaning in life through a new vocation or hobby. Perhaps it is trying to squeeze in all the fun and adventures you put off while you worked your way into retirement. Perhaps it is spending your remaining days with children and grandchildren.

This book explores the issue of finishing well from a Christian and biblical viewpoint. Unfortunately, too many Christians answer the question with the same answers as any non-Christian might. As Christians, we've bought into the idea that prosperity and health and happiness are the measurements of success and the means to fulfillment and a life lived well. For the Christian, however, finishing well should look very different from secular answers. Perhaps there is that small, quiet voice in the back of your head saying, 'Are you sure this is all? Isn't there something else?' The answer is yes.

Here is a quote that can help us answer the question from a different perspective:

> The worth and excellency of a soul is to be measured by the object of its love; he who loveth mean and sordid

things doth thereby become base and vile; but a noble and well placed affection doth advance and improve the spirit unto a conformity with the perfections which it loves.[1]

In other words, what you love most shapes the kind of person you become and the kind of life you live. The quality of your soul and, hence, the way in which you live your life, is measured by what you love most. If you want to measure the worth and excellency of your soul, and by extension, how well you live life, look to what you love, not what you have.

Step outside yourself and look back at yourself. What is it that you love most? You can tell by how you live your life. Don't flinch from such an effort. Don't fool yourself by telling yourself the 'right' answer. Let the choices you make, the treasures you have in your heart, the life you live, tell you what you love most. And we must understand that what we are becoming now is what we will be unless we change our course.

Such exercises are important *because we become like what we love*:

- If I love my pleasures most, I become a worldly person.

- If I love the church most, I become a church person.

- If I love my family most, I become a family person.

- If I love my job most, I become a professional person.

- If I love education the most, I become an educated person.

- If I love Jesus most, I become like Christ.

---

1. Henry Scougal, *The Life of God in the Soul of Man* (Sprinkle Publications 1986, originally, 1677), pp. 62-63.

Consider 2 Corinthians 5:13-15 (NIV):

> If we are out of our mind, it is for the sake of God; if we are in our right mind, it is for you. For *Christ's love compels us*, because we are convinced that one died for all, and therefore all died. And he died for all, that those who live should no longer live for themselves but for him who died for them and was raised again (emphasis mine).

The phrase 'Christ's love compels us' tells it all. What compels you to live the way you do? If it is anything other than Jesus Christ, your life's arc is in trouble. But if your passion in life is Jesus, then your life's arc is upward towards Him. And who you become in this life will be praiseworthy before the throne of God. The end will be excellent.

The secret to finishing as a Christian isn't about the successes. It isn't about greatness. It isn't about the accumulation of great wealth. A poor Christian can finish well. And a rich Christian (or non-Christian), whose love is misplaced, can finish badly. It is how you make your life choices relative to your relationship with Jesus Christ. For the Christian, a life lived well should reflect a gospel-centered focus on living a life of love for the Lord to the glory of the Lord.

'Gospel-centered' means that all the facets of your life are rooted in this wonderful news about a new life in Jesus. Marriage, family, work, recreation, eating, entertainment, service—everything is grounded in a life of grace and the amazing wonder of being set free from the condemnation of our sins and the privilege of living as beloved children of God who love Him back. And it is done not for our glory or gain but for the glory of God.

While the answer of how to finish well is ultimately more complex, **the key for Christians lies in making sure our first and foremost love is rooted in Jesus. Finishing well involves ensuring our love for Jesus is our great**

treasure and living in light of that in all we do and all we are.

It is such a familiar, simple theme, isn't it? And yet, as we move into middle age or older, our passion for Jesus can slip away. We suddenly find ourselves in unfamiliar territory. But there is hope. As long as our life story continues, He is at work in us, He is calling to us, He is for us, He keeps loving us more than we can imagine. He will finish the work begun in us. There is great hope because He loves us so much and He will most certainly glorify Himself in us. It is this God-centered confidence that gives us the courage and conviction to end well.

HOW DO PEOPLE WHO LIVED LONG AGO TEACH US TO LIVE WELL TODAY?

Bobby Clinton, a professor of leadership at Fuller Theological Seminary, studied biblical leaders and made an alarming observation: Of the approximately 800 leaders in the Bible, about 100 have data that allows you to interpret their leadership and about 50 of those allow you to evaluate their finish. He concludes that only 1 in 3 finished well.[2]

This is both stunning and alarming. Some finished well. Others started well but finished badly. And some were bad from beginning to end. No matter how you slice it, the majority, 67 per cent, finished badly. And it will surprise you to see who ended badly. While it cannot and should not be extrapolated to suggest that 67 per cent of us will finish badly, it is still a cautionary statistic that suggests we should be more reflective about our own lives than many of us are. If biblical leaders fail at such a rate, then how much more are we in danger of finishing badly?

---

2. Bobby Clinton, *Listen Up Leaders! Forewarned is Forearmed!* 1989. Clinton lists six traits for finishing well. http://storage.cloversites.com/missouristateassociationoffreewillbaptists/documents/Finishing-Well-Six-Characteristics.pdf

In this book, finishing badly is not saying a person is not saved. Rather, in Paul's description of a person's life in 1 Corinthians 3, finishing badly is like the Christian just escaping the flames:

> If anyone builds on this foundation using gold, silver, costly stones, wood, hay or straw, their work will be shown for what it is, because the Day will bring it to light. It will be revealed with fire, and the fire will test the quality of each person's work. If what has been built survives, the builder will receive a reward. If it is burned up, the builder will suffer loss but yet will be saved—even though only as one escaping through the flames (1 Cor. 3:12-15 NIV)

This book attempts to glean wisdom and guidance from people long dead to see if we can learn from their lives to better finish ours. Their stories, which are often surprising in the conclusion, provide valuable veins of truth that, mined properly, can enrich our stories and help us finish well.

What we will discover is that life stories from thousands of years ago look surprisingly familiar in contemporary times. There are themes and temptations and successes and failures that are common to all men and women in all times. And the hope is that if your story's arc isn't what it should be, then you will find a more God-satisfying, God-glorifying way that leads to the end.

DISCLAIMER

One last note: I am not writing this because I think I am an excellent model for finishing well. I have been a Christian for some forty years. The arc of my life with Jesus has not always been an upwards one as I would define it in this book. I don't have a lot of personal illustrations that say, do it this way if you want to finish well. In fact, I have many more illustrations that say, don't do it this way if you want to finish well. My marriage has had highs and lows. My career is marked by great successes and great failures. So I write this book with quite a bit of humility. My story isn't over yet. We have yet to see if I finish well. I certainly hope I do. And I hope you do too. If this book helps you in some small way to do that, then it is worthwhile for both of us.

So pour yourself a glass of wine (or tea or whatever), have a plate of comfort food, and let's see what these people long gone have to say to us.

1

Caleb

and the Secret to Finishing Well

Everything acts according to the spirit that is in it.
(Charles Spurgeon)

INTRODUCTION

Who is your favorite person in the Bible, excluding Jesus? Let me suggest it is a productive exercise to find someone who speaks to you personally more than most. It's not just intellectual entertainment. That person can shine a light on your own life to help you be more transformed into the likeness of Jesus and to live your life more pleasingly to the Lord.

Caleb from the Old Testament is that person for me. His story is astonishing and reveals the secret to finishing well as a believer. He is my favorite, in part, because his is a story of a long, hard life lived well. It is a fascinating story, for sure. And some of the most important parts of the story don't come until the very end. In old age, Caleb makes a statement that reveals to us the secret to finishing well. This man, as much as anyone in the Bible, can speak to us today and help us finish our race on an upward arc.

THE STORY

Caleb the Slave

Caleb was born at the end of Israel's captivity in Egypt. Having come to Egypt during the great famine in the Middle East, and being received warmly by Pharaoh because of Joseph's plans to save Egypt, Israel is ultimately enslaved by the Egyptians, a situation that lasts 400 years.

Caleb was born near the end of those 400 years. He lived as a slave for 40 years. We know nothing about him during this time but, obviously, he suffered deprivation and a loss of freedom under the slave masters of Egypt. He was born into slavery, grew up a slave as a young man and labored as a slave as a man. Forty years. Imagine such a life. What were his days like? What were his fears and sufferings? What did he dream about?

Something amazing happened during this time. Moses comes with God's power and authority and delivers Israel. Caleb would have been a grown man as this happened. Imagine being among the Israelites at that time. They would have shared stories about the miracles. They would have told each other how Moses confronted Pharaoh himself, calling for their freedom. Imagine the excitement and the fear and the sense of impending danger and change. Caleb would have been caught up in all that too. And then, quite suddenly, they are free. They can go. They can leave. They quickly pack what they already own and what they can take from their masters. And just like that, they are no longer slaves. Caleb's enslavement is over. What a day that must have been.

Caleb the Spy

We first read about Caleb after Israel's miraculous escape from Egypt, capped by the parting of the Red Sea, the safe passage of Israel through the sea, and the destruction of Pharaoh's army. After that, Israel comes to the border of the Promised Land. Moses sends twelve spies into the land to see what is there. One of them is Caleb.

This is a fascinating moment. Caleb is now forty years old. Something must have caught Moses' eye to choose Caleb. Did the Lord tell Moses to select Caleb? Had Caleb distinguished himself some way as a slave that brought him to Moses' attention? We don't know. But here he is. One of the twelve. As it turns out, for good reason.

After forty days, the spies come back; ten give a report of doom and terror. There are many enemies, powerful kingdoms, literal giants. Israel faces sure defeat if they invade. But two of the spies give a different report. One of those spies is Joshua, who will eventually lead Israel in the conquest of the Promised Land. The other is … Caleb.

Here are the competing reports from Numbers 13. First up is the majority report by the ten spies. They tell of the abundance and the great dangers facing them.

> At the end of forty days they returned from spying out the land. And they came to Moses and Aaron and to all the congregation of the people of Israel in the wilderness of Paran, at Kadesh. They brought back word to them and to all the congregation, and showed them the fruit of the land. And they told him, 'We came to the land to which you sent us. It flows with milk and honey, and this is its fruit. However, the people who dwell in the land are strong, and the cities are fortified and very large. And besides, we saw the descendants of Anak there. The Amalekites dwell in the land of the Negeb. The Hittites, the Jebusites, and the Amorites dwell in the hill country. And the Canaanites dwell by the sea, and along the Jordan' (Num. 13:25-29).

The report incites the people. Mass fear breaks out. But suddenly, Caleb stands up and gives another report. This man who has left the land of slavery sees another land. Here is his dissent:

But Caleb quieted the people before Moses and said, 'Let us go up at once and occupy it, for we are well able to overcome it.' Then the men who had gone up with him said, 'We are not able to go up against the people, for they are stronger than we are.' So they brought to the people of Israel a bad report of the land that they had spied out, saying, 'The land, through which we have gone to spy it out, is a land that devours its inhabitants, and all the people that we saw in it are of great height. And there we saw the Nephilim (the sons of Anak, who come from the Nephilim), and we seemed to ourselves like grasshoppers, and so we seemed to them' (Num. 13:30-33).

Twelve men traveling together. Same land. Two very different reports. Only Caleb and Joshua see the land for what it was and Who was going to give it to them. A land flowing with milk and honey. A home for God's people. A promised land. It would take great effort to wrest it from people who hated God and practiced all kinds of evil. But it could be, should be, done.

Caleb is forty years old. He has gone from being a slave in a land of slavery to having seen a new land, and touched and tasted its fruit. He had lived in slavery for forty years. It is likely he knew of the wealth and luxury of Egypt. But he had never tasted it. He knew it wasn't going to be his. However, now … now he had walked a land that was full of promise. He tasted its fruit. Literally. Something happened to Caleb in those forty days. It wasn't just that he had shed his slave life; suddenly, he had seen and tasted the life of a free man in a land of milk and honey. Now he had something to live for that was in his grasp; the promise of such a life that gripped him like nothing else and he would not rest until he returned there.

Caleb the Desert Nomad
Israel's response to the report has terrible repercussions. Rather than embracing the minority report of Joshua and

Caleb, Israel falls into fear and doubt that they can take the land. Due to Israel's unbelief in God's promise and power to deliver the land, God declares that the entire generation of men, twenty years and older, will not enter into the Promised Land; rather they will perish in the desert. Israel is forced to journey for another forty years before they are able to enter into the Promised Land.

> And the LORD spoke to Moses and to Aaron, saying, 'How long shall this wicked congregation grumble against me? I have heard the grumblings of the people of Israel, which they grumble against me. Say to them, "As I live, declares the LORD, what you have said in my hearing I will do to you: your dead bodies shall fall in this wilderness, and of all your number, listed in the census from twenty years old and upward, who have grumbled against me, *not one shall come into the land where I swore that I would make you dwell, except Caleb the son of Jephunneh and Joshua the son of Nun.* But your little ones, who you said would become a prey, I will bring in, and they shall know the land that you have rejected. But as for you, your dead bodies shall fall in this wilderness. And your children shall be shepherds in the wilderness forty years and shall suffer for your faithlessness, until the last of your dead bodies lies in the wilderness. According to the number of the days in which you spied out the land, forty days, a year for each day, you shall bear your iniquity forty years, and you shall know my displeasure." I, the LORD, have spoken. Surely this will I do to all this wicked congregation who are gathered together against me: in this wilderness they shall come to a full end, and there they shall die' (Num. 14: 26-35 emphasis added).

The entire generation of men aged twenty and older who left Egypt, saw the great miracles that freed them from Pharaoh's grasp, saw the parting of the Red Sea—that entire generation of men died out in their desert wanderings. All but two men—Joshua and Caleb.

Imagine what life must have been like for Caleb after this. Having been freed from slavery, having seen a verdant land of almost unimaginable prosperity, he is forced to wander for another forty years. He becomes a nomad. Each day is a day with no permanent home. The days of travel are by foot. They are in desert places. Rocky places. Surrounded by enemies. It is a hard life. For forty more years.

Imagine such a life. So close to the Land. From slave to nomad. What would he have thought after ten years? twenty years? After twenty years, he is sixty. Then he is seventy. And still a nomad. Still wandering. Then thirty-five years. He spends another lifetime, forty years, not having what he longs for. Would he have been angry with God? Bitter at Israel? Would his hope have waned? What did he think as men he knew and worked with died along the way? What were his temptations and fears? How might we have responded in such circumstances?

I don't think we need to idealize Caleb. Surely, there were weary days. Days when he was discouraged. There were days when men he knew, men he had likely befriended, died. Surely he grieved as that happened time and again. Caleb experienced the hardships and privations of life as a nomad. But something also gripped him. In those long years when he faced the physical pain of a long journey, when he faced the heartbreak of losing friends, when he faced the weariness of life, something keep him going. He had tasted and seen. It infused the journey. It didn't keep him from being tired or even fearful. But it kept him focused. Kept him moving forward. Because he was going to taste that fruit again.

Caleb in the Promised Land

At long last, he goes into the Promised Land. The rest of the men of his generation, except for Joshua, have died. Even Moses is gone. But finally, it's time. Time to enter and take the land. We read how they cross the Jordan River in Joshua 3. The priests go ahead and as they cross; the Jordan suddenly parts. And the Israelites pass through.

> So when the people set out from their tents to pass over the Jordan with the priests bearing the ark of the covenant before the people, and as soon as those bearing the ark had come as far as the Jordan, and the feet of the priests bearing the ark were dipped in the brink of the water (now the Jordan overflows all its banks throughout the time of harvest), the waters coming down from above stood and rose up in a heap very far away, at Adam, the city that is beside Zarethan, and those flowing down toward the Sea of the Arabah, the Salt Sea, were completely cut off. And the people passed over opposite Jericho. Now the priests bearing the ark of the covenant of the LORD stood firmly on dry ground in the midst of the Jordan, and all Israel was passing over on dry ground until all the nation finished passing over the Jordan (Josh. 3: 14-17).

What a moment for Caleb. He certainly remembered how the Red Sea had parted as well forty years earlier. First, the waters parted to escape slavery. Now they part to enter the Promised Land. What a thrill. And what a fulfillment of all he has waited and wandered for. At last. At last, he is back ...

With Joshua leading Israel, they cross over the Jordan River and Israel begins its conquest of the land. Jericho is the first city to fall. Israel conquers kingdom after kingdom. Taking the land God has promised is no easy task. It requires battle after battle. And even then, there are temptations after a battle has been won. We will see this later in this book. The point is that in this life every believer must contend for his or her inheritance.

We don't read about Caleb during this time but we know he fought along with the rest of Israel. Even at eighty years of age, he was fighting to take the land.

Caleb and the Secret to Finishing Well

This brings us to the secret of finishing well. To understand this secret, we must hear Caleb's declaration when he approaches Joshua and asks for his specific inheritance of land. The fighting is still going on but the Lord instructs Joshua to apportion inheritances after large territories have been conquered. At that time, Caleb approaches Joshua. He is eighty-five years old. Let's listen to him from Joshua 14:

> Then the people of Judah came to Joshua at Gilgal. And Caleb the son of Jephunneh the Kenizzite said to him (Joshua), 'You know what the LORD said to Moses the man of God in Kadesh-barnea concerning you and me. I was forty years old when Moses the servant of the LORD sent me from Kadesh-barnea to spy out the land, and I brought him word again as it was in my heart. But my brothers who went up with me made the heart of the people melt; yet I wholly followed the LORD my God. And Moses swore on that day, saying, "Surely the land on which your foot has trodden shall be an inheritance for you and your children forever, because you have wholly followed the LORD my God." And now, behold, the LORD has kept me alive, just as he said, these forty-five years since the time that the LORD spoke this word to Moses, while Israel walked in the wilderness. *And now, behold, I am this day eighty-five years old. I am still as strong today as I was in the day that Moses sent me; my strength now is as my strength was then, for war and for going and coming. So now give me this hill country of which the LORD spoke on that day, for you heard on that day how the Anakim were there, with great fortified cities. It may be that the LORD will be with me, and I shall drive them out just as the LORD said'* (Josh. 14:6-12, emphasis added).

Let Caleb's life sink in. A slave for forty years. A desert nomad for forty years. And now, after five years of warfare, he makes this request. 'Give me what I have been promised.

I am eighty-five years old. Still as strong as I was when I was forty. Give me my inheritance that I might drive out the last of our enemies.'

What an incredible declaration! This isn't the declaration of a man worn out by life. It isn't resigned. These are fighting words. These are confident words. This man isn't done.

Here's what this passage is NOT teaching us: Caleb was physically stronger at eighty-five than forty years old. This is not the point of the passage and not particularly helpful to us. What is crucial in helping us is what Caleb is saying beyond the physical: 'I am as zealous to take possession of what God has given me as I was forty-five years ago! I haven't lost sight of my inheritance. I haven't forgotten what I saw. And tasted. It compels me as much today as it did then. Give me what is mine. I was passionate to take it forty-five years ago. I am passionate to take it today. Let's see what the Lord will do with that.'

How are you feeling about your life right now? Does Christ's love still compel you? Are you still amazed at grace? Are you ever more astonished at how high and how wide and how deep the love of God is for you? Does the cross still humble you? Does your life show that?

CALEB'S LIFE EXAMINED AND WHAT IT MEANS FOR US

The secret for the Christian to finish well? It's not about a physical land or any inheritance we might obtain in this lifetime. It's not about physical strength or health at an old age. It's about something much more wonderful, much more amazing. Who can doubt that Caleb finished well? And what made Caleb finish well should sound familiar to the Christian.

1. Caleb had tasted and seen and so have we

Forty-five years earlier, this former slave had seen an unknown land and tasted its fruit and it changed his life forever. When he entered Canaan, he saw a land that captured his heart. A land that God told the former slave, 'This is yours. This is the land that I have blessed and that I give to you. This is the land where you and your family will dwell. With me, your God.' He had seen it, experienced it, walked in it, and tasted it.

What Caleb saw and tasted sustained him for forty-five years. Caleb wasn't overcome by the doubts and fears of others. He wasn't defeated by the long, long march through the desert. He knew what awaited him. When others' faith waned, Caleb's experienced reality in the Lord remained strong. He had seen the land even though it was just for 40 days. Furthermore, it wasn't just about the land. He understood that the Lord was going to be there with him. It was a place to dwell at peace and at home with the Lord. It was worth living for until he received it.

How does that help us today? We have tasted and seen not the fruit of the land but a Person, someone infinitely greater.

Christians aren't simply saved from hell. We get to experience the wonders of being in Christ. Being a Christian is necessarily experiential. And it is something that should surpass any other experience in this lifetime **even though it is only a foretaste**!

Psalm 34 says,

> Oh, taste and see that the LORD is good!
> Blessed is the man who takes refuge in him!
> Oh, fear the LORD, you his saints,
> for those who fear him have no lack! (vv. 8-9)

In this life, we get to taste and see that God is good. Not just good like another good kind of food or drink. Not just good like another pleasant experience or vacation trip. We are in daily, living communion with the living God. Please don't just read through that. Consider and savor this amazing truth. We experience, even if just in part in this life, the wonders of the King of Heaven—a union of power and love and communion in Christ.

These experiences aren't supposed to be small and insignificant. Rightly lived, being in fellowship with God Almighty is the greatest experience of life. There is nothing in this life that compares—not sex, not the choicest food, not the most glorious view of nature, not the most moving music, not the most uplifting speech. Nothing compares to the taste of God in this life.

For all my wanderings in this life, wanderings that sometimes took me away from following Jesus, it is this experienced union in Christ anchored by my salvation by grace alone that holds me. It keeps me from wandering away for good. And it draws me on to the promise that I will one day see Him face to face. Every day offers me the privilege of living in the presence of the living God.

Do I sometimes 'feel' like God is **not** near? Sure. Do I sometimes have doubts that He even exists? Of course. But that has more to do with my forgetting who He is. What I find as I live longer as a Christian is that my relationship takes on the nature of a walk with Him. I don't have to go looking for Him. It is as if we are going on a long walk together. Day in and day out, I talk to Him and He talks to me. I imagine Caleb experienced something like that.

And then there are those singular experiences when God is present in special ways. Powerfully. Lovingly. In His holiness. In His forgiving love. Those moments of awe. Those silencing moments when it would be wrong to even speak. Those times have come when I am surrounded by others in worship and they have come other times when I am by myself. But when those moment come, alone or with others, the overwhelming, holy sense is: The Lord is here. He is present with me right now …

Yes … I've tasted and seen. And it has ruined me from committing to anything or anyone else. Who would want to?

And one more reminder—it's just a foretaste. We won't experience the fullness of being with God until after we die. (See Chapter 9.)

2. He had a different spirit and so do we

There was clearly something different about Caleb. The Lord says as much in Numbers 14 when He utters His judgment against the men of Israel after they refused to go in because of their unbelief from the report of the ten spies:

> But truly, as I live, and as all the earth shall be filled with the glory of the LORD, none of the men who have seen my glory and my signs that I did in Egypt and in the wilderness, and yet have put me to the test these ten times and have not obeyed my voice, shall see the land that I swore to give to their fathers. And none of those who despised me shall see it. But my servant Caleb, *because he has a different spirit* and has followed me fully, I will bring into the land into which he went, and his descendants shall possess it (Num. 14:21-24, emphasis added).

Caleb had a 'different' spirit to him. This bears some elaboration. There is no clear evidence that this indicates that Caleb was filled with the Holy Spirit as a Christian is. It is certainly possible. But in the absence of more clarity from the Scripture, many commentators have chosen to speak of this 'different' spirit as a markedly different character from the other men of his generation. Charles Spurgeon calls it Caleb's 'Secret Character.' 'He had another spirit—not only a bold, generous, courageous, noble, and heroic spirit, but the Spirit and influence of God which thus raised him above human inquietudes and earthly fears.[1]

This 'different spirit' was an internal orientation towards God that caused Caleb to think and act and choose to live a distinguishing life of deep faith and obedience and passion. Caleb's spirit permeated his character and was Godward in its affections and passions and choices. It was a spirit that didn't cave in to cowardice or self-pity or selfish ambition. Surely, when Caleb saw the same enemies that the ten spies saw, he must have realized that Israel could not defeat them on their own. But because his spirit was one of faithful trust in the Lord, he acknowledged the weakness of his own hands only to find the courage needed in the Lord's arms.

We have a different spirit too. In John 3, we read how we've been born of the Spirit. We go through a second birth.

> Truly, truly, I say to you, unless one is born of water and the Spirit, he cannot enter the kingdom of God. That which is born of the flesh is flesh, and that which is born of the Spirit is spirit. Do not marvel that I said to you, 'You must be born again.' The wind blows where it wishes, and you hear its sound, but you do not know where it comes from or where it goes. So it is with everyone who is born of the Spirit (John 3:5-8).

Genuine Christians are born again. They have passed from death to life. They are animated by and indwelt by the Holy Spirit.

That should be prized among all the things in your life. The most amazing miracle you will ever see and experience is your own salvation in which you come alive in Christ with a new spirit, one that cries, 'Abba, Father', one that experiences the great love of the God of the universe.

---

1. Charles Spurgeon, Sermon 538. Caleb-The Man For The Times, *November 1, 1863, https://liveprayer.com/spurgeon-sermons.cfm?s=187203.*

Furthermore, being indwelt by the Spirit gives us a different orientation to the world. It's this same 'spirit' that Caleb had. Consider: We live in a very 'present' oriented society in the United States. Instant everything. And we live in a very self-focused society. What's in it for me right now? Happiness is too often rooted in what we eat and play and enjoy and have and do right now. Unhappiness is based on what we don't have, jealousy over what others have, or what we are waiting too long for or have lost. If Caleb had today's ruling spirit in the West, he would have been a most miserable man for eighty-five years. And I think too many of us are miserable because we've lost our 'spirit' to live for Christ, substituting for it a spirit that seeks immediate worldly happiness and wholeness and pleasure.

Spurgeon goes on to say, 'Everything acts according to the spirit that is in it.'

Finishing well requires a regular recommitment to having a spirit that lives to the glory of God, not the glory of our pleasures. Having received the greatest gift of our lives—our forgiveness, justification, rebirth, adoption and union in Christ—let's not be distracted by the cares and worries of this world, or seduced by the pleasures and desires of this world. Let's have the spirit of a joyful pilgrim and a confident warrior. We've tasted and seen in the past. We taste and see now. Now, let's see it through to the end.

3. It was a God-promised inheritance and we have one too

It wasn't just that Caleb had seen something and was going to take it. This was the Promised Land, promised by God Almighty. And God made a promise specifically for Caleb, as we read in Numbers 14:

> But my servant Caleb, because he has a different spirit and has followed me fully, *I will bring into the land into which*

he went, and his descendants shall possess it (Num. 14:24, emphasis added).

Likewise, Caleb cites Moses in claiming his inheritance:

And Moses swore on that day, saying, 'Surely the land on which your foot has trodden shall be an inheritance for you and your children forever, because you have wholly followed the LORD my God' (Josh. 14:9).

Promises by others are no small thing. They are commitments. Promises by spouses to have and to hold until death do us part. Promises by supervisors to promote. Promises by the government to treat us fairly and justly. Promises by friends to repay debts. Promises play a large part in our lives. But because they are made by human beings, there is never an absolute confidence those promises will be kept, even when they are made in good faith at the time. People change. Circumstances change. But with God, a promise is a sure promise. His very nature—His truthfulness, His justice, His sovereignty—assures us that He will keep His promises. Unlike the promise of anyone on this earth, God's promises are absolutely reliable. And that is something to stake your life on.

Caleb had God's promise. I will bring you into the land. And you and your descendants will possess it. And Caleb believed the Lord. He entrusted his life on that promise. And he lived his life in order to gain it.

We also have a promised inheritance but it is one far more glorious. It is the great hope of glory. There is an inheritance awaiting every believer. As the writer in Hebrews says,

Therefore he (Jesus) is the mediator of a new covenant, so that those who are called may receive the promised eternal inheritance, since a death has occurred that redeems them from the transgressions committed under the first covenant (Heb. 9:15).

We have God's promises that He will keep us to the end. He promises never to leave or forsake us. He promises that the best is yet to come: Eternal life with Him, face to face. In new, glorified bodies built to last forever. In heaven on earth, the new Eden, only better. To grow in an ever increasing and amazing knowledge of God and all He has created in the universe. The little we taste now that is so amazing – it's just a taste. It's not the feast. The feast is promised. It is coming.

Finishing well isn't just focused on how we live here and now. Finishing well as the Christian includes the joyful assurance of God's promises for life after death. The closer we come to death, the more powerful that promise should become. And the more thrilling the anticipation. Lived rightly, embracing God's promise of an eternal inheritance should be the source of increasing joy and expectation as we move into middle and old age.

4. He had an abiding faith and so do we
Let's look closely at this statement from Joshua 14:12:

> It may be that the LORD will be with me, and I shall drive them out just as the LORD said.

This is no waffling statement of faith. It was by faith that Caleb spied out the land. It was by faith that Caleb believed the Lord would deliver their enemies to them as they took the land. It was by faith that Caleb believed the Lord would keep His promise to enter the land. And now, finally, it was by faith that the Lord would help Caleb drive out the last of the Lord's enemies.

This isn't a new believer's faith. This is an old believer's faith. He had seen the Red Sea parted. He had seen the Lord go before Israel for forty years. He had seen food provided from heaven. He had seen water provided when there was none. He had seen the Jordan River part. He knew his God could do it. There is something precious about an old believer's faith. It has been tested and purified. It isn't blind enthusiasm, not that there is anything wrong with enthusiasm. It is time tested. It is relationship tested. It is solid and unshakeable.

Caleb's faith was a living faith. An abiding faith.

We have the gift of abiding faith, too. As Paul writes in Ephesians 2:8:

> For by grace you have been saved through faith. And this is not your own doing; it is the gift of God, not a result of works, so that no one may boast.

It is true that there is a kind of faith that is man-made. It isn't just Christians who have faith in their spouse, faith in a sports teams, faith in themselves to get something done. That kind of faith is a human or self-centered trust in ourselves or others. However, we mistakenly think that saving faith is like that—something we have to generate and maintain. In reality, saving faith, persevering faith, is God-given. It is a gift.

Faith can be a tricky thing. It isn't a once and done phenomenon. It is part of life. It abides only as we feed and sustain it in cooperation with the Holy Spirit. Without attention to it, faith can wane. It can be set aside. Doubts can creep in unchallenged. The faith of forty years ago won't be enough for today. Faith is something renewed by the Holy Spirit. Day by day. Month by month. Year by year. Decade by decade.

The kind of abiding faith that lays hold of our salvation, treasures it beyond everything else, and leads us passionately through this life? The faith that finishes well? It comes from God. And each of us has it.

THE SECRET LAID BARE

What made Caleb finish well was the experience of God's blessing in the form of seeing the Promised Land, tasting its fruits, and believing in, trusting completely, the promise of the Lord to give him that land. Those forty days transformed Caleb to live another forty years of trial and difficulty and five more years of warfare. The taste of the Promised Land and his faith in the Lord energized and enlivened him to persevere through all the temptations, trials and hardship. Clearly, Caleb had treasured what he had tasted and seen and it was the great treasure of his heart.

And therein lies the secret to finishing well for us.

The Christian who genuinely experiences the saving love of Jesus has something far more precious, more life-changing, more glorious than anything else in this life. The source of a compelling perseverance that allows us to finish well is to daily taste and see and live in the crazy, good love of God in the person of Jesus Christ, our Lord and Savior, and to hold on to God's promise that we will one day see Him face to face. It becomes our great treasure. The Christian who grasps this amazing truth, holds it in his or her heart, treasures it, will order and live his or her life accordingly, and will finish well.

The Scriptures return to the wonder of knowing God, of being in right relationship to God, time after time:

> Oh, the depth of the riches and wisdom and knowledge of God! How unsearchable are his judgments and how inscrutable his ways! (Rom. 11:33).

> The LORD is merciful and gracious, slow to anger and abounding in steadfast love. He will not always chide, nor will he keep his anger forever. He does not deal with us according to our sins, nor repay us according to our iniquities. For as high as the heavens are above the earth, so great is his steadfast love toward those who fear him; as far as the east is from the west, so far does he remove our transgressions from us. As a father shows compassion to his children, so the LORD shows compassion to those who fear him. For he knows our frame, he remembers that we

are dust. As for man, his days are like grass; he flourishes like a flower of the field; for the wind passes over it, and it is gone, and its place knows it no more. But the steadfast love of the LORD is from everlasting to everlasting on those who fear him (Ps. 103: 8-17).

This God who created and sustains the universe is ours and we are His. The God who gives us every good thing and who is sovereign over every event that occurs in our lives is ours. The God who justly can condemn us to eternal suffering but instead sent His beloved Son to die for us is ours. Let us absorb this into our inmost being. The Lord is ours and we are His. Nothing comes close to this in life. And this resets everything in life: our treasures, our trials, our successes and our failures. Herein lies the secret to finishing well. And, yet, there is more.

John Piper put it this way:

> Finishing life to the glory of Christ means finishing life in a way that makes Christ look glorious. It means living and dying in a way that shows Christ to be the all-satisfying Treasure that he is.[2]

At the center of the secret

The secret to finishing well isn't just rooted in our experience with God. If it were, it would barely last a day because we repeatedly forget what we have. But it lasts because while we experience the love of God through Christ, God delights and rejoices over us.

John Piper gets to this in *The Pleasures of God*:

> Can you imagine what it would be like to hear God singing? A mere spoken word from his mouth brought the universe into existence. What would happen if God lifted up his voice and not only spoke but sang!

---

2. John Piper, *Rethinking Retirement* (Crossway Publishing 2009), p. 5.

...

What do you hear when you imagine the voice of God singing?

I hear the booming of Niagara Falls mingled with the trickle of a mossy mountain stream. I hear the blast of Mt. St. Helen's mingled with a kitten's purr. I hear the power of an East Coast hurricane and the barely audible puff of a night snowing in the woods. And I hear the unimaginable roar of the sun, 865,000 miles thick 1,300,000 times bigger than the earth and nothing but fire, 1,000,000 degrees centigrade on the cooler surface of the corona. But I hear this unimaginable roar mingled with the tender warm crackling of logs in the living room on a cozy winter's night.

And when I hear this singing I stand dumbfounded, staggered, speechless that he is singing over me—one who has dishonored him so many times and in so many ways. It is almost too good to be true. He is rejoicing over my good with all his heart and with all his soul ... I have it on the authority of the prophet Jeremiah:

> I will give them one heart and one way, that they may fear me forever, for their own good and the good of their children after them. I will make with them an everlasting covenant, that I will not turn away from doing good to them. And I will put the fear of me in their hearts, that they may not turn from me. I will rejoice in doing them good, and I will plant them in this land in faithfulness, with all my heart and all my soul (Jer. 32: 39-41).

Don't run your eyes over the promises of God like the wrong pages in a phone book. God Almighty, Maker of heaven and earth, said, 'I will not turn away from doing good to them ... I will rejoice in doing them good ... with all my heart and with all my soul.' Let all three promises sink in.[3]

What a delicious truth this is: We have been given the most wonderful treasure in the universe: life in and love for Jesus. But more! He treasures us, loves us and rejoices over us.

What is particularly compelling about the love of God for us is this: His love doesn't ebb and flow. His rejoicing doesn't grow weary. His delight over us never diminishes. Because He is the unchanging God, He is unchanging in His love towards us. And if we can lay hold of that truth in our hearts, we can finish well.

Caleb's experience really was a foreshadowing of the life the Christian should live in light of knowing Jesus and being loved by Him. Consider what Paul says about knowing Jesus Christ. In Philippians 3, he calls this life in Christ 'of surpassing worth':

> If anyone else thinks he has reason for confidence in the flesh, I have more: circumcised on the eighth day, of the people of Israel, of the tribe of Benjamin, a Hebrew of Hebrews; as to the law, a Pharisee; as to zeal, a persecutor of the church; as to righteousness under the law, blameless. But whatever gain I had, I counted as loss for the sake of Christ. Indeed, I count everything as loss *because of the surpassing worth of knowing Christ Jesus my Lord* (Phil. 3:4-8, emphasis added).

Imagine that you have something that surpasses the worth of anything and everything else in the world. Would you not live your life a certain way to have and hold that treasure?

To be saved in Christ and then have an ongoing relationship with Him is a high privilege; even more, it is the greatest of all things we could ever have in our life. No one or no thing comes before Jesus in our lives. And if we can grasp this rich, priceless relationship, enter in and ambitiously live

---

3. John Piper, *The Pleasures of God* (Multnomah Press, 1991), p. 187.

in the good of this truth, we can finish well. We can be like Caleb and say in the final season of life, 'My passion for Jesus burns as brightly as it did on the day I was saved. My faith in Him is as strong, if not stronger. My experience of Him is altogether wondrous and unlike anything else in my life. I will press on to take hold of my inheritance in Christ until I go to meet Him. And meet Him, I shall.'

FORGOTTEN TREASURE, OTHER TREASURES, AND STUMBLING BLOCKS

If you are still with me, you are already formulating your objections. To be fair, not many of us will go through life like Caleb, a literal slave, or a nomad wanderer or someone who literally goes to war. Also, as a Christian, you already knew that you are born again, will go to heaven, blah, blah, blah. But maybe you aren't seeing the connection with this and finishing well.

- Maybe you hear Caleb's words and think, 'Nope, not me.'

- Maybe you can't recall ever having a passion for Jesus.

- Maybe you recall a passion and zeal to live for Christ but it has faded into a fond recollection.

- Maybe the idea of tasting and seeing the Lord seems a bit foreign.

- Maybe you have a vague sense that this Christian walk should be different but are too caught up with 'life' to figure out what is keeping you from it.

- Maybe you don't even care to have such a spirit; you just want to get through this life as best you can.

- Maybe, just maybe, you want what Caleb had. Not

a land. But for a life lived passionately before and with your glorious Savior. To the end. And are provoked afresh to consider how to do that.

Unfortunately, for many of us today, Caleb's passion to take hold of his possession of the land far outstrips our contemporary efforts to walk by faith today. It can be quite embarrassing.

- Do I live with this overarching love of Christ that transforms my life?

- Do I live in light of what I have received already and will inherit in full after I die?

Too often, the answer is, 'No.' Instead of living lives in which Jesus is our great treasure, we trade away that treasure for other pleasures, for smaller treasures, and counterfeit treasures, here in this life, without recognizing the harm. And more than that, the trials and tribulations of this life—whether divorce or poverty or prejudice or crime or illness or war or abuse—these too can rob us of our great joy in Christ as well.

A.W. Tozer puts it this way:

> It is my opinion that the Christian concept of God current in these middle years of the twentieth century [he wrote this in 1961] is so decadent as to be utterly beneath the dignity of the Most High God and actually to constitute for professed believers something amounting to a moral calamity.[4]

Do we diminish the value of our God and our salvation? Being saved should be the most wonderful experience in our lives. We may even 'know' that. But is it really? Do we live in the reality of our great salvation, day in and day out, month in and month out, year in and year out?

---

4. A. W. Tozer, *The Knowledge of the Holy* (HarperCollins Publishers, 1961), p. 2.

For some, that treasure isn't such a treasure. If becoming a Christian isn't a compelling experience, then the trials and temptations in our lives will undermine how we live. But be assured, passion for Christ is supposed to be a compelling and hedonistically pleasurable experience that reorders all other pleasures and puts our trials in their proper perspective.

So why is it so often not the case?

Why aren't more of us finishing like Caleb, still passionate for Christ after all these years?

There are stumbling blocks that keep us from having a Caleb-like life. The rest of this book explores a few of those stumbling blocks and counterfeit treasures:

1. What is your treasure in life? Mr. Scougal bears repeating, 'The worth and excellency of a soul is to be measured by the object of its love; he who loveth mean and sordid things doth thereby become base and vile; but a noble and well placed affection doth advance and improve the spirit unto a conformity with the perfections which it loves.' In Chapter 2, taking a hard look at Solomon, we can examine what we truly love and treasure in life. Solomon, who started with what appears to be ideal circumstances spiritually and materially, ends badly because he replaced his first love with a lesser one.

2. Do you think rightly about yourself? If, as A.W. Tozer says, the most important thing about you is what you think about God; the second most important thing about you is what you think about yourself. In the midst of all the ways we evaluate our lives, do we think rightly about ourselves from the Lord's point of view? Many of us are sidetracked from finishing well by thinking unbiblically about ourselves. We may have a clearly defined therapeutic or worldly

idea of ourselves that contradicts how the Bible defines us, burdening us with an inner conflict as to what our ending well should look like. We explore this in Chapter 3.

3. Here is a simple truth: All of us are being either transformed or conformed into something. The story of Lot gives us a simple but valuable measuring rod: are we being transformed or conformed? Lot slowly conformed to the world around him. And the social and psychological pressures of the current age are constantly at work to mold us to a certain way of life. On the other hand, being a Christian means being transformed into someone who is more and more like Jesus Christ. Chapter 4 explores this idea.

4. Properly understood, contentment is one of the greatest treasures of our lives. Chapter 5 explores the idea of a godly contentment amid prosperity and desire. While one might think prosperity is a sure guarantee of contentment, that's often not the case. Using Paul and insights from the Puritan writer, Jeremiah Burroughs, we explore how to live the contented life while challenged by the temptations of prosperity.

5. Are you in danger of falling away? In Chapter 6, we meet Demas, someone who professed faith in Christ, worked alongside Paul himself, but then fell away. We see this happen far too often, and for many it is a secret dread. There are lessons from Demas' life to encourage and caution us in living and finishing well.

6. How does family, church and community help or hinder our finishing? As much as we might like

to think otherwise, we are all parts of groups and tribes, whether family, ethnic groups, political parties or social groups. And these groups can significantly affect the way in which we live our lives and finish. In Chapter 7, Paul's first letter to the Corinthians provides a framework on how to deal with factions and divisiveness.

7. Memorials are not just for the Old Testament. They are milestones and testimonies of the importance of grace in finishing well. In Chapter 8, we look at examples from Joshua as the Israelites conquered the Promised Land. Do we forget what we have and what we are going to receive? How can we create reminders of God's grace in our lives—what He has done, our inheritance in Christ—and how does remembering those evidences of grace increase our faith in this life as we finish? How can we build uplifting reminders of what God has done, what our inheritance in Christ is, and how does remembering what He has done increase our faith as we enter the final stages of life?

8. How compelling is heaven for you? Adam and Eve tell us as much about heaven as Revelation does. The anticipation and reality of Heaven can shape how we live our lives here and now, contributing to an unshakeable joy and anticipation as we approach death's door.

2

Solomon

and Handling our Treasure at the End

It is a blessed thing to love Christ because we escape from hell by Him, it is a blessed thing to love Christ because He has opened the kingdom of heaven to all believers, but it is a still higher thing to forget yourself, and to contemplate with delight the ineffable perfections of Him whom heaven and earth acknowledge to be chief among ten thousand, and altogether lovely. (Charles Spurgeon)

INTRODUCTION

I have a confession to make: I think a lot about money. After both my parents died, we came into a small amount of money. And when both my wife and I were working, we had a large income. Like it or not, we have a good amount of money. OK, I like it. But it changes the way I think and live. On the one hand, we are materially more secure and prosperous. On the other hand, money demands my attention and my affection. Truthfully, the money doesn't demand anything; it's just money. My heart tempts me to love prosperity and wealth over Jesus, a temptation I struggle with continually.

Let me tease this out a bit more. What I've learned over time is that I crave financial security and prosperity. Crave it. It was the hidden foundation of all security in life for me. I uncovered this idol by losing my job as a pastor. And it revealed a serious flaw in my faith. I wish I could say that, as a 'good' Christian and pastor, I immediately trusted the Lord that He would provide for my family and me. I didn't. I was gripped by an irrational fear that I wouldn't find work right away and that our life savings would be drained. It was completely irrational; I remember being almost paralyzed for several weeks. It was not a proud moment ... not even close. And as shameful as my reaction was, what I discovered is that I had a hidden idol in my life. Financial security.

There is nothing wrong with wanting to be financially secure but when it becomes all-controlling, without which life seems to be out of control, then it has moved into the realm of idolatry. Instead of Jesus being my treasure and foundation and my Lord, financial security and prosperity were. Without it, I was miserable, fearful, and anxious.

It has taken a long time to replace financial security as the treasure of my heart with a trust in the Lord. And, truth be told, it is still a work in progress.

The question is, what is your treasure? What do you value so much that your life seems to depend on it? It can be money or investments or real estate. But it can also be other things in life. Non-monetary things. Maybe it is the acclaim of others. The respect of others. Perhaps leisure is your ruling idol. Sex. Drugs. Marriage. Children. Health. Fitness. Friends. Success. Ask yourself, what is in your life that if you lost it, *you* would be lost? There are as many treasures in life as there are people. (And don't be surprised if you can't see it. You may not know what it is until you lose it.)

You will finish well only by rooting out those life-controlling treasures and making sure Jesus is your true treasure.

JESUS AND TREASURE

Jesus helps us tease out this idea about money, wealth, possessions and treasures. In Luke we read:

> Fear not, little flock, for it is your Father's good pleasure to give you the kingdom. Sell your possessions, and give to the needy. Provide yourselves with moneybags that do not grow old, with a treasure in the heavens that does not fail, where no thief approaches and no moth destroys. *For where your treasure is, there will your heart be also* (Luke 12: 32-34, emphasis added).

That last sentence is crucial to finishing well because the battle in our heart over what we treasure is a particular phenomenon as we get older. At some point later in our lives, we have decided we know what is important in life. We've 'earned' what we have. We've paid a price to obtain what we have. Likewise, we put a value on what we have lost. Sometimes our treasure isn't in what we have but what we no longer have. Long-lived lives illumine our treasures in brightly lit ways.

Let's stipulate that we can have many treasures. For our purpose, what we have in mind is the overarching treasure in your heart. What is it that is the crown jewel?

In the movie, *The Hobbit*, the dwarf king, Thorin Oakenshield, seeks to reclaim the kingdom lost when a great dragon drove his people out of their mountain home. In the mountain kingdom is a great horde of treasure—gold and precious gems. But above all of them is the fabled Arkenstone. This is the greatest of all the treasure. And it is this treasure that Thorin Oakenshield lusts after. Without the Arkenstone, he cannot rest.

So what can we glean about how our great treasure, our Arkenstone, affects the arc of our lives? Let's look at someone from the Bible who tragically illustrates the following principles about our overarching treasure: Solomon.

SOLOMON AND THE TREASURE PRINCIPLES

Solomon was King David's son but not the likely successor because of his older brothers Absalom and Adonijah. However, both were killed in rebellion against David and Solomon ascends to the throne.

Solomon was renowned for his wisdom, being called the wisest man of his time. And he was fabulously wealthy, coming to reign at Israel's political and economic zenith. He is credited with writing a major portion of Proverbs, as well as Ecclesiastes and the Song of Songs.

The Good Beginning

Religiously, Solomon began with a deeply personal love of the Lord. We see this when the Lord meets him at Gibeon and asks Solomon what he wants at the outset of his reign. Solomon famously asks for wisdom. However, there is an amazing statement that introduces the story. In 1 Kings 3:3, we read:

> *Solomon loved the LORD*, walking in the statutes of David his father, only he sacrificed and made offerings at the high places (Emphasis added).

This is no small thing. Solomon loved the Lord. This young king started out in a great way with the Lord. Rather than power or victory or fame, he asks for… wisdom. He humbly acknowledges to God that he cannot lead Israel without the wisdom that comes from God and it pleased God that Solomon asked for this. Solomon's start is so promising. Surely, he won't go wrong.

And there is more to Solomon's beginning. The Lord prevents David from building the great temple in Jerusalem, leaving it to Solomon to build. On the day it was consecrated, Solomon was present to see the glory of the Lord fill the temple. It is worth repeating here in light of what will happen later in his life. We read in 2 Chronicles 7:

> As soon as Solomon finished his prayer, fire came down from heaven and consumed the burnt offering and the sacrifices, and the glory of the Lord filled the temple. And the priests could not enter the house of the Lord, because the glory of the Lord filled the Lord's house. When all the people of Israel saw the fire come down and the glory of the Lord on the temple, they bowed down with their faces to the ground on the pavement and worshiped and gave thanks to the Lord, saying, 'For he is good, for his steadfast love endures forever.'

So we have a man who becomes king at the time of Israel's greatest power and wealth, who is renowned for his wisdom and who clearly has a spiritual life of significance, loving God and experiencing God's glory and power personally. In our own modern times, we would say that he had everything he needed to be successful in life and most likely to end well. Immense wealth. A superior education. A strong religious underpinning. Great talents. What could possibly go wrong with such a foundation?

The Bad and Sad Ending
The answer? It all goes wrong. The end is as inglorious as the beginning was glorious. Solomon ends far worse than he began. Ironically, it wasn't his love of money or his great wisdom that ruined him. That's the easy assumption. If it wasn't wealth, then surely he became proud due to his knowledge and wisdom. The betting money would be on one of those two features in his life. But it wasn't. It was

something else that grew and grew and grew until late in life; it ruined him.

The noteworthy passage comes from 1 Kings 11:

> *King Solomon, however, loved many foreign women besides Pharaoh's daughter—Moabites, Ammonites, Edomites, Sidonians and Hittites.* They were from nations about which the LORD had told the Israelites, 'You must not intermarry with them, because they will surely turn your hearts after their gods.' Nevertheless, Solomon held fast to them in love. He had seven hundred wives of royal birth and three hundred concubines, and his wives led him astray. *As Solomon grew old, his wives turned his heart after other gods, and his heart was not fully devoted to the LORD his God, as the heart of David his father had been.* He followed Ashtoreth the goddess of the Sidonians, and Molech the detestable god of the Ammonites. So Solomon did evil in the eyes of the LORD; he did not follow the LORD completely, as David his father had done (1 Kings 11:1-6 NIV, emphasis added).

Where was Solomon's great treasure at the end? It turns out it wasn't in the Lord. Even though Solomon loved the Lord as a young man, the great treasure of his heart at the end turned out to be the love of foreign women. Not only did he take many wives and concubines, but they came from other lands that worshipped other gods. And it shaped his life. How? Over the years, as he acquired more and more wives and concubines that love of women was the fertile soil for full blown idolatry. Idolatry had been growing all along as the number of women grew. And the great love in his heart led him to worship other gods as well.

The Scriptures Tell the Story

As noted earlier, Solomon was the author of Proverbs and Ecclesiastes. These books really trace the arc of his life.

While there is no way to accurately date when the Proverbs were written, their content argues for

Solomon's earlier life when his passion was still for the Lord. They speak of the fear of the Lord as the beginning of all wisdom. They paint the picture of Lady Wisdom and Lady Folly and how they contend for the hearts of men and women. They warn of foolishness, pride and lust, all which come into bloom later in Solomon's life. And Proverbs 31 celebrates the godly woman. The book doesn't appear to be written by a man with 1,000 wives and concubines. It is a properly celebrated book of wisdom for believers.

On the other hand, Ecclesiastes reflects the sad tale of a king at the end of his life. And, like Solomon, the book is uninspired in the end. It begins with the conclusion, 'Vanity of vanities, says the Preacher, vanity of vanities! All is vanity.' It points out the meaningless of life. And its best line, hardly inspiring, comes at the end in chapter 12:

> The end of the matter; all has been heard. Fear God and keep his commandments, for this is the whole duty of man. For God will bring every deed into judgment, with every secret thing, whether good or evil.

While true, this is not a stirring call to faith. Is that really the end of the matter? The gospel offers far more than that. This sounds more like Paul's description of one escaping from the fire ending in 1 Corinthians 3.

Some commentators work hard to see the gospel and a positive message in Ecclesiastes. I think it is better understood when read in light of the end of Solomon's life. Ecclesiastes, as a book, has a cautionary message, revealing to us the effect when we trade a love for and trust in God with a love for worldly pleasures and trust in other gods. There is no suggestion that Solomon goes to hell. But it does suggest that his finish is as sad as his beginning was joyful.

BUT I'M NOT SOLOMON ... AM I?

At first glance, Solomon's story is so different from ours. He was a king and he had 1,000 wives and concubines. The number is astonishing and repellant. We think to ourselves, I would never be that kind of person.

Or would we?

We may not have 1,000 wives and concubines but we do have lots of lovers calling us away from Jesus. Not literal lovers. But loves, big and small that call to us, entertain us, seduce us. Take video games or social media like Facebook. They are intentionally designed to draw you in and keep you. Think of the hours you spend in front of a screen, living and breathing a virtual world that is not real.

You don't play video games? How about sports? Or TV? Or eating? Or wine? Or shopping? Or traveling? Or sex? Or gambling? Or pornography? What pleasures do you allow yourself that rob you of your time and will and desire? Oh sure, they aren't big idols in your life; they are just ways to enjoy life. But what happens if the power goes out? What happens if the game is cancelled? When we can't get our fix of worldly pleasures, life is boring or worse, meaningless. Our happiness is far too rooted in these 'foreign wives and concubines.'

No, we may not be like Solomon with 1,000 women giving him sexual and emotional pleasure but we seem to be doing quite well finding our own 1,000 'foreign women' that lead us away from loving Jesus. In our own little kingdom of 'Me', maybe we aren't so different from Solomon after all.

Let's look at three principles that can be gleaned from Solomon's life that help us measure how far astray we might be and how dangerous that is to finishing well.

Your treasure grows over time

It is quite likely that had we asked Solomon in his early years as king if he thought he would follow other gods, he would have laughed out loud. He was David's son. He had spoken to God face to face. He built the great temple in Jerusalem. He had seen the glory of the Lord fill the temple. Follow other gods? Impossible. Except the seed was planted due to the real treasure in his heart. The love of idolatrous women.

We don't know for sure what Solomon thought as his heart was pulled away from following the Lord (although the book of Ecclesiastes gives us a good idea). What we do know is that the treasure in his heart, his Arkenstone, was the love of idolatrous women. And it grew over time. And in the end, it ruined him as he turned from the Lord to follow other gods.

The point: The more treasure you have, the more you have to love. And what you love shapes your choices and actions.

Over time, most people find that their financial investments have grown. Their houses become more valuable, notwithstanding periods of recession. Their stock market portfolio grows. Their retirement account increases.

In the same way, our other treasures' value and importance grow in their own way. If your job is your great treasure, you likely are more and more successful. If your family is your treasure, it has grown, either because you have more children or grandchildren or because your children are older with more experiences. If your spouse is your treasure, then that love has grown.

Once that treasure catches us and then increases in value, it drives us to make decisions good or bad. Solomon started with one wife and ended with 1,000 wives and concubines. His great treasure started out small (one foreign wife) but finished big. What about you? What treasures started out small but now have grown into life significance to you?

If we want to finish well, no other treasure can supplant our love for Jesus. Instead, He must be the Arkenstone, the great treasure without which we know we cannot live. And our life should reflect a growing love for Him. What starts as a small seed of faith and relationship needs to be cultivated and cared for and nurtured. If Jesus is the great treasure of your heart, that love will grow over time. Maybe the passion will ebb and flow, but, over time, at the end, you will have so much more of Him. And it will shape all of your decisions and choices the entire course of your life.

Your treasures become more precious to you over time

Related to this idea of increasing treasure, over time the things you treasure become *more important* to you. The treasure in your heart doesn't just increase with its own effect. Its importance grows. So not only does your treasure increase, so does your attachment to it.

In J.R.R. Tolkien's *The Hobbit* (the book, not the movie), Bilbo encounters the dragon who has laid up all the treasure it has stolen over the years. The dragon loves its treasure. Its treasure is the true meaning of the dragon's life. Read how the treasure blankets the dragon:

> There he lay, a vast red-golden dragon, fast asleep; a thrumming came from his jaws and nostrils, and wisps of smoke, but these fires were low in slumber. Beneath him, under all his limbs and his huge coiled tail, and about him on all sides stretching away across the unseen floors, lay countless piles of precious things, gold wrought and unwrought, gems and jewels, and silver red-stained in the ruddy light.
>
> Smaug lay, with wings folded like an immeasurable bat, turned partly on one side, so that the hobbit could see his

underparts and his long pale belly crusted with gems and fragments of gold from his long lying on his costly bed. Behind him where the walls were nearest could dimly be seen coats of mail, helms and axes, swords and spears hanging; and there in rows stood great jars and vessels filled with a wealth that could not be guessed.

To say that Bilbo's breath was taken away is not description at all. There are no words left to express his staggerment, since men changed the language that they learned of elves in the days when all the world was wonderful. Bilbo had heard tell and sing of dragon-hoards before, but the splendor, the lust, the glory of such treasure had never yet come home to him. His heart was filled and pierced with enchantment and with the desire of dwarves; and he gazed motionless, almost forgetting the frightful guardian, at the gold beyond price and count.[1]

This dragon didn't simply have a treasure horde, an immense amount of treasure. And he didn't just love his treasure. It was an essential part of the fabric of life itself.

This description challenges us. Is Jesus such a treasure in our hearts? Do we drip with the love of and for Jesus? I think Caleb would have understood that description easily. He would have said, 'Yes, the land where God will dwell with me, that I've been promised, is like that.' Shall we not say the same and more about the glorious Savior who knows us and loves us with a love that is so wondrous?

The Point: The more precious your treasure, the more you are invested in it. The extent to which your treasure takes you away from Jesus, the less you will be invested in the gospel, the church, and the Kingdom of Heaven, but most of all, Jesus Himself.

John Piper in *Life is a Vapor* spoke of the 'coronary Christian' as the Christian whose heart is fully committed in a great cause. They are not adrenaline junkies who

---

1. J.R.R. Tolkien, *The Hobbit* (Ballantine Press, First printed 1937, Fiftieth Printing 1974), p. 206.

have a spurt of energy and then grow tired. The heart of the coronary Christian beats on and on for the cause they live for.

> Oh for coronary Christians committed to great causes, not great comforts. I plead with you to dream a dream that is bigger than you and your families and your churches. Un-deify the American family, and say boldly that our children are not our cause, they are given to us to train for a cause. They are given to us for a short season so we can train them for the great causes of truth and mercy and justice in a prejudiced, pain-filled, and perishing world.[2]

Following on that description, let me suggest that there is a kind of coronary Christian who isn't simply committed to great causes. He or she is devoted to loving Jesus and being loved by Jesus in a deep and profound way. To be such a coronary Christian, Jesus must become more and more precious to you over the span of your life. Ultimately, living with and for Jesus, is the great cause. When Jesus is the great treasure in your heart, you are given over not just to live for Him but to live *with* Him. Day by day. Until the end comes. And when it does, people will say, 'Oh, his/her treasure was Jesus!'

Your last days reveal your true treasure

We saw with Solomon that it was in the last days that his real treasure came into its fullest expression and its most ruinous effect, leading him into idolatry.

Here is a parable in Luke 12 that speaks to how the last days reveal our treasure.

> Someone in the crowd said to him, 'Teacher, tell my brother to divide the inheritance with me.' But he said to him, 'Man, who made me a judge or arbitrator over you?' And he said to them, 'Take care, and be on your guard against all covetousness, for one's life does not

---

2. John Piper, *Life is a Vapor* (Multnomah Publishers, 2004), pp. 62-63.

consist in the abundance of his possessions.' And he told them a parable, saying, 'The land of a rich man produced plentifully, and he thought to himself, "What shall I do, for I have nowhere to store my crops?" And he said, "I will do this: I will tear down my barns and build larger ones, and there I will store all my grain and my goods. And I will say to my soul, 'Soul, you have ample goods laid up for many years; relax, eat, drink, be merry.'" But God said to him, *"Fool! This night your soul is required of you, and the things you have prepared, whose will they be?" So is the one who lays up treasure for himself and is not rich toward God'* (Luke 12: 13-21, emphasis added).

What a cautionary parable! How many of us will be surprised at the moment that we are called home in death. Will we be drawn up short because our treasure isn't in meeting Jesus face to face but in the treasures we had laid up here on earth?

It appears that until the Lord called the man in the parable home, he had no idea what his treasure really was. I am sure that if he had been asked if he loved the Lord, he would have said yes. He wasn't called an evil man. It might even be assumed that the Jews listening to this parable thought of the man as a godly man. There was nothing wrong with being wealthy.

But while he wasn't called an evil man, he dies being called 'foolish' as he enters eternity. And he enters eternity in poverty.

Death, or its impending arrival, reveal our hearts in ways that we often cannot see. These events can open a window, albeit briefly, into our own hearts.

My mother loved her grandchildren. I can still remember her hearty laugh when they would visit her and say those grandchildren things that only grandparents can appreciate. She was quite well off after a lifetime in which she and her husband had stewarded their investments. After my father died, she and I would take care of giving the annual birthday gifts. She would give each grandchild a gift of money. And therein is a tale. There were six grandchildren. And each one would get $10. So $60 a year. It made me laugh because she could give much more. And as the children got older, $10 to a teenager wasn't really much. But that was the amount. Over time, I was able to talk her up to $100. But then something interesting happened. As she got much older, and sicker, the amounts went back down until it was only $1. When I mentioned this to her financial advisor, he told me something I've always remembered. He said that was common among old people. It wasn't so much the money as the fear of loss of control. All she had control over at the end was her money and she was afraid to let it go. And isn't that true for us all? We all want to be in control, even when we see ourselves losing control. Control is a huge treasure.

What have death and illness revealed to you about what you really treasure? Is it material security? Prosperity? Health? Family? Or is it Jesus? As you get older, your treasures should come more into focus. And their importance to you may or may not become more apparent to you. Don't assume they will. But it will be apparent to you on the other side.

JESUS IS THE TRUE TREASURE BUT ...

Here is the core of finishing well: Jesus is the true treasure, the Arkenstone. Paul understood this and prayed the following for believers in Ephesians 3:

> For this reason I bow my knees before the Father, from whom every family in heaven and on earth is named, that according to the riches of his glory he may grant you to be strengthened with power through his Spirit in your inner being, so that Christ may dwell in your hearts through faith—that you, being rooted and grounded in love, may have strength to comprehend with all the saints what is

the breadth and length and height and depth, and to know the love of Christ that surpasses knowledge, that you may be filled with all the fullness of God (Eph. 3:14-19).

There is nothing like knowing the love of Christ. Nothing compares.

That said, there is a twist: Christians know this already. We know the right answer but, if we are honest, it is often not apparent in how we live our lives. Take a minute to evaluate how you treasure Jesus versus how you treasure other things in your life. It is very possible that you have substituted other treasures. Here are some questions to examine yourself by:

- Does your life look like someone who treasures Jesus?

- Is your personal relationship with Jesus growing so that He is more real to you than ever?

- Is Jesus more and more precious to you?

- Do hardships and losses reveal that Jesus truly is your great treasure?

Two cautions emerge for those who are older:

First, are you living off the 'interest' of your knowledge of Jesus? In other words, you have a certain amount of treasure in Jesus. But as you grow older, instead of adding to the investment, do you live off the interest of what you know about Jesus? You've had your big moments with Jesus. You have your stories and they comfort and encourage you. But that is your story. It's the learning and living from the past.

Second, is Jesus part of a mutual fund of treasures? A mutual fund allows you to 'own' shares in many companies, while minimizing your risk because you aren't invested too heavily in any one stock. Is it that way with Jesus, who becomes one of many treasures instead of the great treasure? Of course you love Him. But you also love your leisure and your friends and your family and food and, and, and … All those treasures are bundled up so no single one is too risky. It comforts you to know that you are being wise by living well across a spectrum of pleasures and treasures.

WHAT DOES TREASURING JESUS LOOK LIKE?

We were made to treasure something. God made us that way. So it's not a simple matter of denying our heart's inclination to treasure something. In other words, you can't help treasuring something. This is akin to Calvin's observation that the heart is an idol-making factory. What matters is what or who we treasure.

What does treasuring Jesus look like? It is the man or woman who fully and exhaustively delights in being with Jesus, walking with Jesus, living for Jesus, talking to and about Jesus, giving his or her all, to become rich in the knowledge of Jesus.

It doesn't mean some constant 'high' or emotional enthusiasm. Some of the most powerful moments in which I treasured Jesus came at my lowest moments in life. Weakness, depression, loss, and suffering can unmask our love of Jesus like nothing else in life. To finish well is a life's walk with Him as the center of our mind and heart. Day by day. Season by season. Never letting go. Never being let go of by Him. Just like Caleb did for those forty years.

Charles Spurgeon urges us to live lives that are won over by the love of and delight in Jesus:

> It is a blessed thing to love Christ because we escape from hell by Him, it is a blessed thing to love Christ because He has opened the kingdom of heaven to all believers, *but it is a still higher thing to forget yourself, and to contemplate with delight the ineffable perfections of Him whom heaven and earth acknowledge to be chief among ten thousand,*

and altogether lovely. 'We love Him because He first loved us,' here we begin, and this beginning always remains, but on it we pile tier after tier of precious stones of love, which are crowned with pinnacles of inexpressible affection for the great Lord Himself. He in Himself has won our hearts, and carried our spirits by storm, and now we must do something which will express our love to Him. That love is not only a gratitude for benefits received from Him, *but an intense affection for His glorious, adorable person. Come, dear friends, do you feel that kind of emotion in your hearts at this time?* Do you even now feel that so perfectly has Christ won the verdict of your understanding, so completely has He bound in silken fetters every movement of your affections that you need to be doing something which shall have but this one aim, to express your love to Him who has made you what you are? *Indulge the emotion, crown it with action, and continue it through life.* [3] (Emphasis added.)

A life lived well to the end piles 'tier after tier of precious stones of love, which are crowned with pinnacles of inexpressible affection for the great Lord Himself.' It is going through life with an ever increasing experience of living with the love of Jesus in all things. All our highs and lows. All our failures and successes. Until our last day.

Jeremiah Burroughs wrote *A Treatise on Earthly-Mindedness*, which was published after his death in 1649. I can't recommend it enough. Listen to how he describes treasuring God and compare it to how you think of God.

It is a heavenly principle that God, the infinite First Being, is infinitely worthy of all love for Himself. The saints in heaven look upon the infinite excellency and glory of God, they look upon Him as the First Being of all things, having all excellency and glory enough to satisfy all creatures

---

3. Charles Spurgeon, *To Lovers of Jesus – An Example*, A sermon given on April 12, 1885, http://www.spurgeongems.org/vols31-33/chs1834

forever. They look upon Him as infinitely worthy of all love and service for Himself.[4]

Who talks like that today? Who thinks like that? About God? We should. And more than think that way, we should believe it and feel it in our inmost being and it should radiate out into all we do. God is worthy enough to satisfy us forever. There is the secret to finishing well.

Let's keep reading Mr. Burroughs:

> 'Communion', you will say, 'what's that?' By communion with God we mean the acting of the soul upon God, and receiving the influence of the goodness, love and mercy of God into the soul. When there is a mutual acting of the soul upon God and God upon the soul, there is a mutual embracing and opening of hearts one to another, for the satisfying of one another's spirits. It is as when friends have communion with one another, that is, when one acts for the comfort of one another. So communion with God is the mutual acting of the soul upon God and God upon the soul in return. The saints see the face of God and God delights in the face of the saints. They let out their hearts to God and God lets out His heart to them.[5]

In this lifetime, we taste and see the first fruits of communion with the living God. And even though they are just the first fruits, the Christian who does so experiences the delight of God, Himself. We let our hearts out to God and He lets out His heart to us. There is nothing else like it.

And let's finish with this from Mr. Burroughs:

> I remember it was written of Queen Mary, that she said if they ripped her open they would find tea in her heart. And so it may be said of saints whose conversation is in heaven, who walk with God and live here lives of heaven

---

4. Jeremiah Burroughs, *A Treatise of Earthly-Mindedness* (Soli Deo Gloria Publications, Third printing 1994), p. 94.

5. Burroughs, *Ibid*, p. 95.

upon earth, if they were ripped open you would find heaven in their hearts.

Suppose God were to come this moment and rip up all your hearts, revealing them to all the men of the world. What filthy stuff would be found in many of your hearts? But for those whose conversations are in heaven, they would be ready to have God rip open their hearts whenever He pleases, 'Lord, Lord, try me, search me, examine and see what is in my heart!'[6]

Want to finish well? Be like Queen Mary. Come to love Jesus, delight in Him, and experience His delight in you so that if you were ripped open, they wouldn't find tea or material treasure or video games or vacation homes or lots of money or work or even family. They would find the greatest treasure in the universe—Jesus.

A FEW EXAMPLES

All that may sound a bit unrealistic. Here are some examples of how that might look in real life.

Certainly practice the spiritual disciplines of prayer, reading, worship, meditation, etc. You won't have as rich a relationship unless you take the time to be with Jesus in a focused way. These disciplines help you in that regard.

But in addition to the disciplines, cultivate an awareness of Jesus being with you all the day long. Simply remind yourself that He is there with you all the time. When you are at work. When you are driving. When you are on vacation. When you rise in the morning and go to bed at night.

Remember that your emotions may ebb and flow, that your circumstances will change, that you will suffer in life as well as prosper but that your treasure remains the same. One of the great ways to treasure Jesus is to remember that He is ever present: In your times of abundance. In your

---

6. Burroughs, *Ibid*, p. 98.

times of need. In your sadnesses and your joys. Too often, we make the mistake of moving away from God based on our circumstances when He wants to draw us closer and closer in all circumstances.

Learn to talk to Jesus. Burroughs called it having a 'heavenly conversation.' Too many of us only communicate with Jesus when we pray. That consumes a precious small amount of time on a daily or weekly basis. A relationship involves ongoing conversation. Talk to Him. Throughout the day. You will be surprised how much you can be engaged with Him. And learn to listen to Him. Not that you will hear a human voice, but learn to sense what He wants you to know.

Practice seeing God in all that happens in your life. Good and bad. He is the sovereign God. Nothing happens apart from His sovereign will. See God at work in your work, your family, your commute, your shopping. And He is at work for your good. A pastor once transformed traffic jams for me. He suggested that we see traffic jams as proceeding from God's sovereign control. Your response is up to you. Get angry and frustrated. Or see it as the opportunity to pray for people. Hahahaha. There's a transforming moment. I fail as many times as I succeed at that. But if you can do it, it draws you closer to your God. And changes your heart a little bit more.

Learn more about Him. One of the reasons we fail to treasure Jesus is that we don't have a rich storehouse of knowledge about Him. Here's a good test: What do you know a lot about? Do you know more about your work than Jesus? More about a sports team or athlete or celebrity than Jesus? More about a city or country? More about computers and software? More about tea or coffee? If you do, you don't know Jesus well enough. Put down your phones, get off social media and find books that tell you about Jesus in depth. And then begin to think about

Him more and more. You will spend eternity learning about Him after you die. If you want to finish well in this life, start learning more about Him now. Here are just two examples of the many fine books about Jesus. Read John Stott's *The Incomparable Christ* and Peter Lewis' *The Glory of Christ*. You will be amazed at how much there is about our wonderful Savior.

Go to church with a particular mindset. According to one study back in 2013, while more than 40 percent of Americans 'say' they go to church weekly, it turns out than roughly 20 percent are actually in church. In other words, more than 80 percent of Americans are finding more fulfilling things to do on weekends. If you are a Christian and you are not going to church, start going again. And if you are only going once in a while, start going weekly. Moreover, too often we go to church expecting to receive from God. Go to church planning on giving glory to God during worship. Go to church primarily to give thanks. Go to church expecting to meet Him. Go to church understanding He delights in meeting with His people. Have the expectation that you will come out of church more aware of your great God than when you went in. Practice going to church to give God honor and praise and be surprised how much you get in return. Go to church. Remember the Sabbath.

Practice the law of love in your life. If Jesus is your true, great treasure, then the love He has for you will spill over into love for others. 1 Corinthians 13 summarizes the qualities of love that should manifest more and more in your life:

> Love is patient and kind; love does not envy or boast; it is not arrogant or rude. It does not insist on its own way; it is not irritable or resentful; it does not rejoice at wrongdoing, but rejoices with the truth. Love bears all things, believes

all things, hopes all things, endures all things. Love never ends (1 Cor. 13:4-8).

Is this what others see in your life? A life of patience and kindness? A lack of rudeness? A life that is not irritable? A life that rejoices with the truth? And does this flow from a life of being loved by Jesus? Finishing well means loving Jesus for sure but others, including our enemies, as well.

CONCLUSION

If you examine yourself and find yourself lacking, it's not too late. Start now. Don't put it off. Solomon started off well. He 'loved the Lord.' He ended practicing idolatry and doing 'evil in the eyes of the LORD.'

We don't have to be like that. If you were to write your reflections about life, would they be more like Proverbs? Or would they sound more like Ecclesiastes? The Lord, our God and our great Friend, is always calling us to Himself. Regardless of your age. Regardless of your estate. Regardless of past failures or sins. It is in this communion with God, a living faith in God, a willing obedience to God that our treasure in Jesus grows and grows. It is not too late to finish well. No matter how old you are.

3

Thinking Rightly

About Ourselves Just as Jesus Did

What comes into your mind when you think about God is the most important thing about you. (A.W. Tozer)

INTRODUCTION

I mentioned at the beginning of this book that the source material came from a series of messages given on Sunday mornings at the beach with a group of friends. We are all roughly the same age and moving more and more into that dreaded land of senior citizenship.

It's not as bad as it sounds, mostly. After all, isn't 60 the new 40? But in recent years, our age is catching up with us in serious ways.

- Jean is in remission from breast cancer
- Donna has suffered from a bad back
- Leo lost his hearing in one ear
- Diane had major eye surgery
- Glenn injured his neck
- Su had a foot injury that hobbled her for almost two years
- I have had a blood clot in each leg

- My wife has had six operations on her eyes for glaucoma and cataracts

And then there is Tommy. Tommy is a great guy. He would tell you he wasn't the brightest light in school. And he was short in stature. But he was an athlete, playing football, baseball and golf. A natural and successful salesman. Passionate and full of life. Friendly to everyone. A continual stream of stories and jokes. Humble. Passionate. A loving husband who would tell you that he married up when he married Jeanie (and he did.) He was a great father who made his mistakes raising his sons like we all do but left no doubt that he treasured his boys. And he was an 'all in' Christian.

Several years ago, Tommy was diagnosed with Alzheimer's. He talked about it that next time we all came to the beach. And we all cried. We prayed for him. And his wife. He came one more time but that was the last time he came. The disease is slowly taking him over. He's still there but it is now obvious. And it makes me cry as I write this. Maybe you can think of someone you know like Tommy. Or maybe, just maybe, you are Tommy.

Coming to the end is hard. It doesn't mean you can't finish well. But it is hard.

This chapter has a very simple message. More of a reminder perhaps. As we get older, we see changes in ourselves and among ourselves—physical, mental, emotional. And who knows what else is to come? It deepens questions about our mortality. How soon? What will it be like? How will I respond?

And so this simple message is about thinking clearly about ourselves as the end nears, as we all prepare to go home, whether soon or years from now.

THE SECOND MOST IMPORTANT THING ABOUT YOU

Have you ever wondered what the most important thing about you is? One of the most powerful quotes I have ever read answers that question:

> What comes into your mind when you think about God is the most important thing about you.[1]

It's important because what you think about God shapes your worldview, your understanding of the meaning and purpose of life. It determines your choices. If you don't think much about God or don't think He is deeply involved in your life, you live your life a certain way.

If you believe in God but don't think rightly about God, it will affect how you live for Him. But the more accurately you think about God, the more you think deeply about Him as He describes Himself, then the richer and deeper your life is in Him.

That's the most important thing about you.

If this is true, then I think *the second most powerful thing about you is what comes into your mind when you think about yourself.* 'Who am I?' is second only to 'Who is God?'

And as we get closer and closer to the end of our lives, I think it is ever more important for us to think as biblically correct about ourselves as we can.

WHAT DID JESUS SAY ABOUT HIMSELF?

No one was more clear about who He was than Jesus.

From the very beginning, others questioned who He was. John the Baptist sent disciples, asking, 'Are you the one who is to come, or shall we look for another?'

---

1. A.W. Tozer, *The Knowledge of the Holy* (HarperCollins Publishers, 1961), p. 1.

(Matt. 11:3) The devil challenged Jesus in the desert, 'If you are the Son of Man ...' (Matt. 4:3). The Chief Priest and elders questioned who He was, 'By what authority are you doing these things, and who gave you this authority?' (Matt. 21:23) And even at the end, Pontius Pilate asks, 'Are you the King of the Jews?' (Matt. 27:11)

While everyone around Him debated whether He was a fraud, a fool or the Messiah, Jesus was secure in Himself. Secure enough that He could prepare the disciples for after He was gone. Consider His dialogue with Peter in Matthew 16:

> Now when Jesus came into the district of Caesarea Philippi, he asked his disciples, 'Who do people say that the Son of Man is?' And they said, 'Some say John the Baptist, others say Elijah, and others Jeremiah or one of the prophets.' He said to them, *'But who do you say that I am?'* Simon Peter replied, 'You are the Christ, the Son of the living God' (Matt. 16:13-16, emphasis added).

Jesus isn't asking this because He doubted Himself. He knew He was the Son of the living God. There was nothing to prove. There was no one to impress. He was who He was—I AM.

Again and again, Jesus answers the question, spoken or unspoken, 'Who am I?'

I am the good shepherd (John 10:14)

I am the bread of life (John 6:35)

I am the light of the world (John 8:12)

I am the resurrection and the life (John 11:25)

All that Jesus did in this life was grounded in His clear, unwavering, unassailable, true understanding of who He was. It stood the test of false accusations and the doubt of the masses. But it drew others to Him because of the truth of what He said about Himself.

Jesus' example must be our own. Just as Jesus was secure in who He was, so should we. We cannot afford to let others define us. And we must be clear headed in our own thinking if we are to finish well. When we can rightly answer that same question, 'Who am I?', our lives change. Dramatically.

ANSWERING THE QUESTION

The question, 'Who Am I?' is more relevant than ever to believers in the West. The rise of the leisure class, the rise of the therapeutic mindset, the rise of ethnic and national pride—they all compete for our psychological and emotional allegiance and self-identification.

The reality of that answer is often more murky and less simple because we often aren't as honest with ourselves as we might like to think we are.

(And at the outset, let me apologize if any serious philosophers happen to be reading this. I am not going to delve into deeper teleological or ontological questions, be it existentialism or post-modernism or whatever. Those conversations have their place but, frankly, I am not qualified to swim with you in those depths. I did read Sartre's *Being and Nothingness* back in college. Honestly, I would like those weeks of my life back.)

Think of a shopping cart. Instead of filling it with groceries, you are going to fill it with what you think about yourself and how you define yourself:

- You can look at your ethnicity and nationality.
- Certainly there are roles—husband/wife, father/mother, grandfather/grandmother.
- There is your personality—outgoing, shy, curious. A thinker? A doer?

- Maybe you've taken a psychological test like Myers-Briggs—you are an ESTJ or INFP or ENTJ or one of 16 other classifications …

- There is more to be added to the cart: What are some of the controlling instincts that cause you to live the way you do? Pride? Jealousy? Sexual immorality? Generosity? Gentleness? Humility?

- And what else? Do things of the world fill up your cart too? A lifestyle of comfort, affluence, certain toys like video games? Convertible cars? For myself, I think there would have to be included a large screen TV.

When you look at the cart, is it full or are there only a few things? And what are the most important things in the cart? Could it be that having too many things in the cart overwhelms what is important?

What's in the cart can begin to help you answer the question, 'Who am I?' The answer begins to emerge based on how we think about ourselves and how we live. We may or may not like the answer. But rather than a theoretical answer, the simple truth is that the shopping cart points to a functional reality about who we are.

Yet there are limitations to this approach. Because as much as we look hard at ourselves, we often simply cannot see the most important things about ourselves.

WHAT IS THE BIBLE'S ANSWER?

As it evolves more and more rapidly to a humanistic and non-eternal worldview, contemporary Western culture says that who we are is rooted in a temporal and immediate lifestyle that allows us to choose to be whoever we want to be. The answer to 'Who am I?' goes something like this, 'You are simply a creature who should live in the here and now, living to be as happy as you can, being whoever you want to be.'

The Bible has a very different answer than modern Western culture. The Scriptures tell us how to fill that cart. Here are seven ways that the Bible describes Christians in terms of their identity. There are more, of course, but these are of particular note relative to Jesus. And all are critical to finishing well.

Saints (Holy Ones)
Philippians 1:1 says,

> To all the saints in Christ Jesus who are at Philippi, with the overseers and deacons ...

The Greek here for 'saints' simply means holy ones. That's who we are. Holy ones. R.C. Sproul helps us with understanding this:

> Christians in the early church were called saints. Since that time, the word *saint* has undergone strong changes in our vocabulary. Now the word *saint* conjures up images of a super-righteous person, a person of extraordinary piety and spiritual power. The Roman Catholic church has made it a title for those who have been canonized into a special list of spiritual heroes and heroines.
>
> The Bible uses the word saint for the rank-and-file believer. In the New Testament all of the people of God enjoy the title *saint*. The word simply means 'holy one.' The New Testament saints were the holy ones. It seems odd that the term is used for believers who were struggling with all sorts of sins. When we read the epistles of Paul, we are struck by the fact that he addresses the people as saints and then goes on to rebuke them for their foolish and sinful behavior.[2]

---

2. R.C. Sproul, *The Holiness of God* (Tyndale House Publishers, 1985), p. 237.

Sproul goes on to explain that holy has two meanings and is applicable to both God and believers. First, it carries the sense of being set apart. While God is set apart in His transcendence, we are set apart to glorify God as His chosen people. Second, it carries the meaning of perfect righteousness. We are both set apart for God to become perfectly righteous but we have also been justified, that is, made perfectly righteous, by Jesus' death on the cross. The writer of Hebrews gets to this when he says, 'For by one sacrifice he has made perfect forever those who are being made holy' (Heb. 10:14 NIV).

One of the most amazing transactions when we are saved is that Jesus' perfect holiness is credited to us … forever. Intrinsic in the nature of a Christian is that they are already perfectly holy through the imputed holiness of Jesus. In that way, you are as holy as you will ever be. At the same time, you are also being made holy by putting off sin and putting on righteous qualities such as love, peace, humility, kindness, etc. All this while you are already as perfect as you can be.

If you are a Christian, you are a saint, a holy one. That's especially important to know as regrets over past sins and mistakes add up. It is an ever present necessity to remind ourselves that we are saints because, if we pause to tally up our sins as we grow older, the need for our salvation in Jesus only increases. We discover that the debt Jesus had to pay was much greater than we imagined when we were first saved. And that gift of justification—being declared righteous in Christ—is far more wonderful than on the first day we were saved.

Let the fact of being a saint make you ever more grateful in old age, as you approach the end, than when you were first saved. And let it free you to push ahead to the end with faith and love and self-sacrifice.

Friends of Jesus

Jesus says in John 15:15,

> No longer do I call you servants, for the servant does not know what his master is doing; but I have called you friends, for all that I have heard from my Father I have made known to you.

Think of your best friends. What makes them so? They are compatible, trustworthy, accepting, loving. They aren't subservient. They aren't strangers. They are on the 'inside' of you. They make your life better, more enjoyable, richer.

Here's a most amazing declaration by Jesus. We are His friends. He has chosen to enjoy us forever as His friends. To share eternal life in a bond of friendship. We will go through eternity with Him, enjoying Him and being enjoyed by Him as friends.

More so, how did you become friends with God? It isn't because He needed your friendship. And we certainly didn't earn His friendship. Besides, that's not how true friendship comes about. He has decided that you will be friends with Him. He simply chose us. We love because He first loved us.

What a comfort this truth is as we enter the final stretch. It is rare to have lifelong friends. If you have them, thank God right now. Most of us have lost our good friends over time. I do not have childhood friends with me anymore. And some of the most meaningful friends I had earlier in life have simply moved on. Some friendships were lost due to my sins or theirs. I am blessed to have dear friends now. But I have one Friend who has been with me all along. Jesus. And more still, His friendship only grows more and more. While He has known me through and through, I discover more about Him as a friend as I grow older.

And here is one final, important, comforting truth when we come to the end of our lives: We discover what kind of friend we have in Jesus. He stays with us as we end. Jobs end. Health fails. Eyes grow dim. Beauty fades. Strength decreases (sorry, Caleb). Friends fade. But He is ever more our friend. He doesn't excuse our sin; instead, He stands with us, calling us onward. He doesn't give up on us. When we can't run, He walks with us. And when we can't walk, He sits with us, or carries us.

Want to finish well? Lean on Jesus, your great friend.

Children of God the Father
1 John 3:1-3 (NIV) says,

> See what great love the Father has lavished on us, that we should be called children of God! And that is what we are! The reason the world does not know us is that it did not know him. Dear friends, now we are children of God, and what we will be has not yet been made known. But we know that when Christ appears, we shall be like him, for we shall see him as he is. All who have this hope in him purify themselves, just as he is pure.

Think of that. We are children of God, the almighty, holy, loving, sovereign God. He doesn't just create a people of His own. He doesn't just call us friends. He creates His family, a family for eternity.

All of us have family histories. Some are dear and precious and the idea that we are God's children is easy to grasp and embrace. God genuinely is our Father, a loving father. Others of you don't have good family histories. Whether by divorce or abuse or neglect or whatever, the idea of being children in a family isn't necessarily appealing. When considering the idea of being His children, it may take a little more work for you to grasp, but it is a fruitful labor.

I didn't have a bad family history but maybe this might help those of you who struggle with the notion of family and children. I didn't have an expressive father. I knew he loved me but there wasn't much physical affection or expressions of love. He worked hard, he put me through college, he was there. But the idea of an expressively loving father was somewhat foreign to me. In fact, later in life, I took great pleasure in hugging my dad and telling him I loved him, which often made him squirm. But I knew he liked it too.

This is what helps me. The passage in 1 John says God 'lavishes' His love on us. God, my father, isn't like my natural dad. He is altogether different. To lavish love means love in generous or extravagant quantities. And that love is not conditional, it doesn't vary, and it isn't temporary. God loves you intimately and personally, like a father, in generous and extravagant quantities. I don't relate God to my father. I relate to God my father in a completely different way. And it is a joyful and amazing thing. It might take time to get used to but it's the truth, and a powerful truth at that.

Brothers of Jesus
Romans 8:29 says,

> For those whom he foreknew he also predestined to be conformed to the image of his Son, in order that he might be the firstborn among many brothers.

I have the best brother in the entire world. He is eight years older than me. We hardly spend any time together. But I love him and think he is the best. He has accepted me over a lifetime of stupid choices, self-pitying moments, and unwise living. He has watched out for me. Taken care of me in critical moments. Stood with me when my father died. Stood with me when my mother died.

But it turns out that I have an even better brother—Jesus. This notion of being brothers is important. Brotherhood done well bonds us together. We are joined as brothers with Jesus in relationship to the Father. This is a truly remarkable relationship. If you've neglected being brothers to Jesus, I suggest you make it a point of emphasis. He is not far away. He is not just the King of Kings. He is not just the Great High Priest in heaven interceding for you. He is all that but at the same time He is also your brother. Your flesh and blood brother. You will spend eternity with Him. And when He sees you, He won't greet you as a stranger or a servant or a creature. He will greet you with great love and affection as your brother.

Slaves of Righteousness
Romans 6:16-18 asks,

> Do you not know that if you present yourselves to anyone as obedient slaves, you are slaves of the one whom you obey, either of sin, which leads to death, or of obedience, which leads to righteousness? But thanks be to God, that you who were once slaves of sin have become obedient from the heart to the standard of teaching to which you were committed, and, having been set free from sin, have become slaves of righteousness.

The idea of being a slave can be an insulting one to the contemporary reader. Certainly, slavery in the West carries terrible, horrible connotations. So we need to understand what Paul is saying here. The Bible is making clear that we aren't moral free agents. We are either slaves to sin or slaves to righteousness in the sense that our internal bent is either to engage in sin in all ways or we are bent to righteousness in all ways.

The bad news is that non-Christians are slaves to sin. No matter how hard they try to be good, and in a relative way they can do much good, their efforts are always tinged with sin. Think of it this way. If you bake a brownie—a delicious, rich brownie—but put just a teaspoon of dog manure in the mix, the entire brownie is ruined. It's that way with being slaves to sin; sin will always ruin efforts to do right.

But to be a slave to righteousness means that we are no longer naturally bent towards sin, towards wrong-doing. We are not sinners. We are saints who sin but sinner is not our fundamental identity anymore. Instead, our fundamental orientation is towards righteousness. We love it. We want it. We pursue it. We grieve when we miss the mark. But we cannot rest until we are fully righteous.

Again, this is so important the older you get. There are certain besetting sins, I call them 'life sins' that we struggle with our life-long. And it is discouraging at times to be engaged with the same sin patterns over years and decades. Maybe it is pornography. Or gluttony. Or jealousy. Or gossip. Or greed. Or laziness. For you who are older in life, as you deal with the sin in your life, knowing you are a slave to righteousness keeps you from falling into despair. It keeps you from giving up.

Furthermore the more I grow in righteousness and the more I can glimpse God's holiness, the more I seem to see the bad left in me. It's a challenge. The temptation is to conclude that there is nothing good in me. For all the good I've done, there seems to be more failure. But Paul wants to remind us: as new creations in Christ, we are full of goodness (Rom. 15:14). Our fundamental bent isn't to do evil, it's to live holy lives as slaves of righteousness. That is our new identify.

Living Sacrifices
Romans 12:1 says,

> I appeal to you therefore, brothers, by the mercies of God, to present your bodies as a living sacrifice, holy and acceptable to God, which is your spiritual worship.

The notion of living sacrificially is an almost heretical notion in Western culture. Possibly psychotic. This culture esteems prosperity and accumulation. That's certainly true of the Boomer generation. Even if you are a Gen X or

Gen Y or any of the follow-on generations, there are things to acquire.

But the Christian is meant to be a living sacrifice. What does that mean? Sacrifice implies that something of value is given up for something greater. It is an act of giving for the sake of something or someone greater. Our entire life is supposed to be given up to Jesus. To live the Christian life is a radical break with this present Western culture. And it is helpful to embrace it as you get older. As we've pointed out earlier, our treasures and wealth grow as we get older. If we aren't living sacrificially, we begin to horde that treasure. But to give our lives and treasure away in love? We are most Christ-like when we do so. We become more like Jesus, who left His throne and came to earth as a sacrifice for our sins that we might be reconciled to Him.

What does it look like to be living sacrifices? One way is to evaluate how you handle your treasures. Do you hoard them for yourself or do you give them away out of love for Jesus? Think of time, wealth and reputation, big treasures all, and how they suggest a living sacrifice.

- Do you give your time to go to church and have fellowship with other believers?
- Do you give your time to serve others?
- Do you give your wealth in joyful, abundant offerings to the church or ministries that help others?
- Do you give your wealth as blessings to others, especially to those in need?
- Do you risk your reputation by standing clearly for the gospel at work, with friends, with family?
- Do you risk your personal reputation by being expressive worshippers?

If you are older, stop and take stock. Are you living more and more for yourself? Or more and more for Jesus? What's the arc, the trend line? A life lived well should 'smell' more and more like a life of spilled perfume. There should be a fragrance that comes from a life lived for and with Jesus that fills the air around you. You should feel poured out. And people should know God through the fragrance of your life.

If that's not you, it's not too late. It may be harder to live this way if you haven't done it or done it recently, but it's worth it. And can be done.

His Sheep
In John 10:27 Jesus declares,

> My sheep hear my voice, and I know them, and they follow me.

In the pantheon of God's creatures, sheep are not the first you look to for inspiration. I remember a friend preaching a cautionary message about the stupidity of sheep. They can be stupid, following each other off a cliff. They are defenseless against predators. And they are prone to wander off and get themselves into trouble.

However, recently, there has been a movement to rescue a sheep's reputation. In a 2016 BBC article, a number of studies were cited showing sheep to be smart, resourceful and playful. Turns out, it's ok to be a sheep. [3]

And there are qualities about sheep that speak to us as Christians. Joe Thorn cites Thomas Watson in an article for The Gospel Coalition that sheep aren't stupid and lists the qualities of value about sheep.[4]

- Sheep are innocent—Sheep aren't harmful creatures; they're harmless and peaceful.

---

3. Harriet Constable, 'Sheep Are Not Stupid and They Are Not Helpless Either' (BBC Earth, April 19, 2017), http://www.bbc.com/earth/story/20170418-sheep-are-not-stupid-and-they-are-not-helpless-either

4. Joe Thorn, 'Sheep Aren't Stupid' (The Gospel Coalition, February 26, 2016, https://www.thegospelcoalition.org/article/the-sheep-arent-stupid/).

- Sheep are meek—Sheep are meek creatures who know their place and willingly submit.
- Sheep are clean—Sheep look for green pastures and search out clean water.
- Sheep are useful—Every part of a sheep is useful. Its meat, its wool, and its skin are offered up for the good of others. In a similar way, the whole life of a believer is useful.
- Sheep are content—A sheep will 'feed upon any pasture where you put it,' Watson observes. 'Put sheep upon the bare common—and they are content. They feed upon the little they pick up in the fallow ground, a perfect emblem of true saints who are the sheep of Christ. Let God put them into whatever pasture He will and they are content.'
- Sheep are timorous—Finally, a sheep is timid. 'It is very fearful if any danger approaches,' Watson notes. 'It is easily frightened by the wolf. Thus the saints of God, who are Christ's sheep, pass the time of their sojourning here in fear. They are fearful of provoking God; fearful of wounding their peace; fearful of temptation; fearful they should come short of heaven through sloth.'

In that light, consider how the Bible describes His people like sheep who are shepherded and protected by the Great Shepherd. And we know His voice.

What is true about sheep and us is that they and we need a shepherd. And we need to recognize His voice. The voice leads us to safety and pasture. The voice warns us of danger. The voice finds us when we are lost. Furthermore, the shepherd sings to His flock, He speaks to them, comforts them, and loves them.

What an amazing truth. So many people in this life think they must go it alone, that there is no one watching out for them, guiding them, protecting them, leading them to provision. That is not the situation for the Christian.

'My sheep know my voice.' Here is a true statement about you. You know the voice of God. He speaks to you. And you follow Him.

In modern culture, with social media and podcasts and hundreds of channels of television and movies and streaming songs, there is a cacophony of voices competing for our attention. As you live your life, it is worth asking yourself, 'Whose voice do I listen to?' While there are many voices calling to us, if we stop and listen, one voice in particular is calling out to us among the rest. The one voice we all know. Your Shepherd is calling out to you and we know His voice.

A test to see if you are finishing well is to ask yourself, to whom am I listening? The more we listen to Jesus, the more familiar we become with His love, His direction, His correction and encouragement. It's not a voice that we only hear from time to time. His voice is the voice of a friend who has traveled long with us. And the voice provides more and more comfort as the aches and pains and sorrows of old age take root in our lives. If you are finishing well, the voice of your shepherd is clearer and louder and more comforting than ever.

CAN WE EMBRACE THE TRUTH?

Consider what these seven names and statements say about us:

Three of these statements point us towards what we are and what we are becoming. And all are oriented towards God Himself; that is, our identity as expressed in these concepts speak to who we are relative to the Father.

- Righteous
- Sacrifices
- Holy ones

The other four talk about being in a relationship. As Christians, our identity is rooted in a personal relationship. We are not solitary creatures. We are not alienated. We are made to live in fellowship with God and also with each other. And so we are:

- His sheep
- His friends
- His children
- His brothers

The answer 'Who am I?' for the Christian is completely bound up in relationship before God. We may say other things. We may listen to other voices. We may have other ideas. But the truth is, this is who we are when we are saved. And this is who we will be for eternity.

Embracing this shapes how you live your life. If these truths mean more to you than your ethnicity or your nationality or your social status or your educational background status or your work or your family, you live your life accordingly. When we answer the question, 'Who am I?' these ways, then we make decisions and live our lives rooted and flourishing in this connection to Jesus. It radically transforms how we live life.

Too often, as Americans, our first question in a relationship, be it work or marriage, or in a church or organization, is 'What do you want me to do?' Or 'What am I supposed to do?' It's about doing. Those questions need to be asked. But when it comes to who we are as Christians, the first question is, 'How do I relate to God as His sheep, his friend, his child, his brother?' Only then should we ask, 'Now how does God want me to live?

If we are to finish well, we absolutely must get the answer to who we are right.

THREE EXAMPLES OF WHY THE RIGHT ANSWER IS IMPORTANT

Since this book is addressed primarily to Christians, let me give several examples of why getting the answer to who we are is so important. There are many ways to mislead ourselves as to our true identify. Even wrong theology can mislead our lives.

'I am a Sinner'

Over the years, some Christians, including myself, have had a word to describe ourselves: 'Sinner.' I would call myself a sinner when it came to my identity. And I was in good company. Many Puritans did the same. Where does it come from? From our awareness of indwelling sin before a Holy God. We know God is holy. And as we pursue holiness in our own lives, we see this remaining sinfulness and it torments us. We read in Romans 7:16-25:

> Now if I do what I do not want, I agree with the law, that it is good. So now it is no longer I who do it, but sin that dwells within me. For I know that nothing good dwells in me, that is, in my flesh. For I have the desire to do what is right, but not the ability to carry it out. *For I do not do the good I want, but the evil I do not want is what I keep on doing. Now if I do what I do not want, it is no longer I who do it, but sin that dwells within me.* So I find it to be a law that when I want to do right, evil lies close at hand. For I delight in the law of God, in my inner being, but I see in my members another law waging war against the law of my mind and making me captive to the law of sin that dwells in my members. Wretched man that I am! Who will deliver me from this body of death? Thanks be to God through Jesus Christ our Lord! So then, I myself serve the law of God with my mind, but with my flesh I serve the law of sin. (Emphasis added.)

It is a confounding dynamic. Furthermore, as we draw closer to God, as we become more sanctified, as we see our sin more clearly, as we perceive His holiness better, we seem to see ourselves as ever more sinful, and it is ever more grievous to us. J.C. Ryle explains this phenomena:

> The nearer (the Christian who pursues holiness) draws near to God's holiness and perfection, the more thoroughly is he sensible of his own countless imperfections ... The brighter and clearer is his light, the more he sees of the shortcomings and infirmities of his own heart. When first converted, he would tell you he saw little of them compared to what he sees now.[5]

But that does not make us sinners. It is one thing to be distressed at the sin we struggle with as Christians. It is another to call ourselves sinners because of it when there is no explicit biblical warrant to call ourselves sinners. In fact, as we have seen, we are saints, not sinners. Our identity is the opposite.

Why highlight this? First and foremost, we need to lay hold of how the Scriptures explain our identity. If the Scriptures preclude it, then we must preclude it too. Secondly, calling ourselves sinners can make us prone to defeatism, discouragement and depression. We think we can never overcome any particular sin. We give up on ourselves. For those of you who struggle like this, stop calling yourselves sinners. Sinning saints? Sure. But not sinners. That is why our identity becomes even more important as we get older. As the debt of sin grows, we can be defeated by the ongoing battle. We can be discouraged over our seemingly constant failure to live rightly before God. We can become depressed over a seeming inability to conquer sin. But that is believing a series of lies. Want

---

5. J.C. Ryle, *Holiness* (Charles Nolan Publishers, 2001), p. 105.

to finish well? Remember who you really are. And keep fighting the fight of faith, just like Caleb.

'I am an Addict'

We are witnessing the rise of an addiction society that may be unmatched in history. Addictions are as old as humanity, but these days we are experiencing a societal embrace of addiction on a scale that is hard to take in, due, in my opinion, to the spread of prosperity to so many without a matching moral guidance on how to deal with prosperity. In other words, an enormous number of people no longer have to struggle to eat and feed themselves; instead, they live in a world where they have the means to indulge themselves with addictive pleasures. And it comes with the decline of moral guidance on how to deal with those pleasures. Whether it is an addiction to alcohol, pornography, gambling, video games, television, drugs, sex, or food, it seems that the societal moral warnings and restraints advocated against compulsive and harmful behavior have been removed.

In response to these powerful forces, there have been therapeutic prescriptions that, while effective to some degree in combatting these social scourges, have in themselves a potentially dangerous seed of their own. Starting with Alcoholics Anonymous, a panoply of therapeutic programs have arisen that are based on an honest embrace of the compulsive behavior, the acceptance of the need for the help of a higher power, and the reliance on a community of like-minded individuals to reach and maintain sobriety.

Please understand that I have a high regard for these programs, particularly those that are rooted in some degree of Christian or biblical underpinnings. I know people personally who have been part of these programs and I believe their testimonies of the dramatic changes that have been achieved in these programs. The practical good cannot and should not be disputed. Lives have been wonderfully and even radically improved. All one has to do is hear the desperate and tragic stories of how addictions have ruined lives and families to know these programs offer a miraculous opportunity for escape.

However, there is a difference between honestly owning the addictive behavior as opposed to tying your identity to that addiction. 'I am an alcoholic' is a confession of having been seduced by the power of alcohol. Honest confession, whether you are religious or not, is a crucial first step to change. For the Christian, however, 'I am an alcoholic' is the wrong answer in terms of answering the question, 'Who am I?' Jesus did not die for us to be a recovering alcoholic or pornography addict or glutton. He died for us to be much more.

This may seem to be an intellectual quibbling over words, but it is far more important than that. It is one thing to say to God, 'I am an alcoholic.' It's another thing to say, 'I am your son (or your daughter) and you have broken the power of sin in my life.' It runs the risk of saying there is a greater power than God. And it runs the risk of believing that addictive captivity is what defines us.

There are many good Christians who have gone through these programs and love Christ deeply and profoundly and live God-glorifying lives. The men I am thinking of who have gone through these programs are far better Christians than I am. But there are others whose dependence is not on the Lord but upon the program. And more, there are some Christians who live defeated lives, still struggling with their addictions, having bought into a false identify. 'I am an addict' becomes a brick wall that separates them from the abundant life in Christ. Something is wrong there.

'God didn't die for junk'

The self-esteem phenomenon of the past thirty years has its own perverse manifestation in the minds of some Christians. Google the phrase, 'God didn't die for junk' and you will read article after article that denies that we simply are too wonderful as human beings for God not to die for. As one pastor wrote, 'Humanity is the pinnacle of his work, and God in creating us didn't create junk!'

In one sense, the above sentence is true. God didn't create junk when He created Adam and Eve. They were without sin. They were the pinnacle. But they didn't even finish their own lives without a species-wide change from something wonderful to something worse than junk in God's eyes. Junk is something that is worthless, no longer of use. But we don't curse junk. Adam and Eve were banished from the Garden of Eden under a curse.

The Scriptures completely contradict the claim that we are somehow intrinsically worthy of being saved. Here is a sampling:

And Jesus said to him, 'Why do you call me good? No one is good except God alone.' (Luke 18:19)

For from within, out of the heart of man, come evil thoughts, sexual immorality, theft, murder, adultery, coveting, wickedness, deceit, sensuality, envy, slander, pride, foolishness. All these evil things come from within, and they defile a person. (Mark 7:21-23)

The heart is deceitful above all things, and desperately sick; who can understand it? (Jer. 17:9)

Have mercy on me, O God, according to your steadfast love; according to your abundant mercy blot out my transgressions. Wash me thoroughly from my iniquity, and cleanse me from my sin! For I know my transgressions, and my sin is ever before me. Against you, you only, have I sinned and done what is evil in your sight, so that you may be justified in your words and blameless in your judgment. Behold, I was brought forth in iniquity, and in sin did my mother conceive me. (Ps. 51: 1-5)

For God so loved the world, that he gave his only Son, that whoever believes in him should not perish but have eternal life. For God did not send his Son into the world to condemn the world, but in order that the world might be saved through him. Whoever believes in him is not condemned, but whoever does not believe is condemned already, because he has not believed in the name of the only Son of God. And this is the judgment: the light has come into the world, and people loved the darkness rather than the light because their works were evil. For everyone who does wicked things hates the light and does not come to the light, lest his works should be exposed. (John 3: 16-20)

Indeed, Jesus didn't die for junk. He died for a people who were existentially wicked and disobedient. Junk is simply used up and good for nothing. We were violently and intractably opposed to Him and as such, we were objects of wrath. Who gets wrathful at junk? He didn't die for junk. He died for His enemies. We deserved judgment. But instead, we received mercy. That's what makes the cross and grace so amazing. He didn't die because of anything inherently good in us. He died for us out of grace alone and a decision on His part to love the unlovely.

Such thinking undermines the glorious truth in the hymn, 'Amazing Grace.' Consider the lyrics,

Amazing Grace, How sweet the sound
That saved a wretch like me
I once was lost, but now am found
T'was blind but now I see

Such thinking would have no place in the world of high self-esteem. Grace is no longer amazing if God saw something worth dying for. Perhaps there would be a hymn, 'Of Course, Grace!' Of course God would die for me. That makes sense and it means I have always had worth in God's eyes. It may not be amazing but it makes sense. The only problem? That's not the truth.

Why is this so important? If we hold to the notion that there was something worth dying for, we miss the glory of the good news. We miss the amazing truth that who we are now in Christ is nothing short of the greatest miracle in our lives.

Do you want to finish well? Make 'amazing grace' a truth, a daily reflection, and an object of amazement. It never gets old. Jesus died for you when you were His enemy and there was nothing good in you. That's amazing. It will change not only what you think about yourself and how you live your life, it will enrich your relationship with Jesus like nothing else.

WHAT ARE THE BENEFITS?

There are plenty of benefits for getting this right in this life. In his book *Heaven on Earth* Thomas Brooks provides a list of the benefits of the assurance of our salvation.[6] The list is equally valid for helping us embrace who we are biblically.

- It creates a great admiration of God's love and favor in Christ. Even when we think about ourselves, we see God's love and grace at the root of it and this causes us to think more about Him.
- It causes the soul to seek a fuller enjoyment of God and Christ. Not just think about Him but enjoy Him more.

---

6. Thomas Brooks, *Heaven on Earth* (Banner of Truth Trust, 1961, Reprinted 1996) pp. 288-297.

- It is usually frequently assaulted by Satan. It is an axiom. Think more biblically about who you are and Satan resists you more.
- It makes the believer bold. When you genuinely think these things about yourself, you are less afraid of what others think.
- It makes the believer seek the happiness of other men. Ironically, thinking biblically about yourself causes you to think more about others and how to be a blessing to them.
- It strengthens the believer against all sin. It is still a battle.
- It is attended by love, humility and joy. When we think of ourselves as sheep, children, brothers and saints, the goodness of God fills us and shapes us.

All of these add to a life lived richly at the end.

THE FINAL BENEFIT

But here's a final thought:

This notion of knowing who and what we are is most important as we prepare for our last day.

On the day we die, we go alone.

We may be with family and friends at the very end. My brother was with my dad. My wife was with her dad. But we may be alone. My mother died alone at night in a nursing home.

Regardless of who is there at the end, we will cross over by ourselves. No one goes with us. It will go dark here. And we will awaken at that moment to heaven.

The friends and family we have here won't be there. They will be back here.

All of your fame and accomplishments that might make you think well of yourself? They won't go with you.

All of your wealth and possessions that give you security? All of your worldly pleasures? They won't be there.

When we go to heaven, we leave this world behind. Literally.

But you. You will be in heaven. All at once. It will be a strange place but you will be more at home there than anywhere here. We don't know what happens. Will there be friends waiting for us? Family? Angels? Jesus? What will anchor us in those first few minutes is this:

- I know who my God is.
- I know who I am.

These two important truths about us will lead us over. These two important truths about us will make the passage more secure. More safe. More exciting.

And that's the most important reason to be clear about this now.

Thinking rightly about yourself brings many benefits in this life. You experience more peace, you are able to fight sin better, and you can develop a rich and fruitful relationship with Jesus and others. But for all those benefits, it is that moment of walking into eternity when right thinking will matter most.

CONCLUSION

Teenagers often adopt personas of people they admire. Maybe it is a celebrity or sports figure or actor or teacher or parent or other adult. They are trying to answer the question, 'Who am I?' Over time they shed those personas and grow into a more personal sense of identity. Maybe they are secure in that identity, maybe not.

As believers, we do something of the same. Before our salvation, we were like those teenagers, trying on different personas. But once we were saved, the Word of God began clearing out all the wrong thinking about who we are. We don't shed personas; we shed false notions of ourselves. And in their place, the truth of who we are becomes more and more clear. Made in the image and likeness of God, we find eternal truths about who we are.

When we do that, something powerful happens. The clearer we understand who we are, the more confident we live in this life. It doesn't matter so much what others think. That's a wonderful security from external psychological pressures. But I think that knowing the truth of who we are is even more valuable to the internal psychological pressures in our own heart. For all the accusations and self-judgments and historical conclusions we make towards and about ourselves, knowing who we really are becomes a plumb line of truth, enabling us to live more God-pleasing, God-glorifying and God-satisfying lives as we approach that day. We no longer fall prey to the debilitating self-statements that simply aren't true about us any longer. Unlovable? Not anymore. Unforgiveable? Not anymore. Hopeless? Not anymore. Irredeemable? Not anymore. Slaves to sin? Not anymore. Alone? Not anymore.

Let's give thanks that our Jesus, who knew who He was on earth, has revealed Himself to us. But He also wants us to be secure in who we are in Him, making that truth the foundation for the rest of our lives.

4

Conformed or Transformed?

Learning from Lot

Ironically, this is how temptation comes in. Violate your conscience a little bit today and a little bit more tomorrow; read the Bible a little less today and just a little bit less the next; pray a few minutes less today and a few minutes less tomorrow; witness a little less today and but a trifle less the next day. This is how you slide backward. Satan will not have you stop gathering, reading the Bible, praying or witnessing all at once. No, he will instead cause you to draw back little by little. He is most patient in pulling you back only gradually. (Watchman Nee)

INTRODUCTION

There is a constant tension inside every Christian. Not a physical tension, although sometimes it can feel like it. But there is an emotional, intellectual, and, ultimately, a spiritual tension. Paul identifies it in Romans 12:1-2 (NIV):

Therefore, I urge you, brothers and sisters, in view of God's mercy, to offer your bodies as a living sacrifice, holy and pleasing to God—this is your true and proper worship. *Do not conform to the pattern of this world, but be transformed by the renewing of your mind.* Then you will be able to test and approve what God's will is—his good, pleasing and perfect will. (Emphasis added.)

The tension we experience on a daily basis, however much we are aware of it, has to do with the change we experience as believers to become more Christ-like. However, the change is a battle—between conformity to this world and transformation into being more and more like Jesus Christ. Too many of us fail to see that the transformative work of the Holy Spirit is a lifetime's work. We aren't saved and done. And we don't 'arrive' in old age. The pull between the Spirit and our old self with its love for this world goes on until the day we die.

Here are questions we should be asking as we grow older:

- Are we being continually transformed into the image and likeness of Jesus or are we being conformed into the image of the culture we live in?
- Can we see ourselves becoming more and more kingdom citizens whose values and purpose in life are directed more and more towards Jesus the King?
- Or are we slowly being conformed more and more to a life that looks like that of anyone else, both on the outside and inside?
  - o Esteeming love of ease, comfort, affluence, love of food, love of wine?
  - o Valuing productivity and morality as ends in themselves?
  - o Preferring external beauty over internal beauty?
  - o Getting our ethics from society rather than God's Word?

Paul warns us: Don't be conformed. Don't do it. Be aware. Be alert. It can happen. You aren't immune from it. And, frankly, we know it's true. As we grow old, we know that there are strong currents that pull us towards the world, away from the Lord. In this chapter, we are going to look at the life of a believer from whom we all could learn a lot—Lot.

LOT AND THE BIBLICAL EXAMPLE OF CONFORMITY

Many of us know the short version of Lot's story. He is rescued from Sodom by angels when the Lord judges and destroys Sodom and Gomorrah. His wife turns into a salt pillar when she looks back as they are fleeing.

What you might not remember is that Lot earlier offered his daughters to the lecherous crowd in Sodom that wanted to have sex with the angels who had come to rescue Lot and his family. And Lot would later get drunk and pass out while his daughters engaged in sex with him to get pregnant. And the offspring of that immoral union would give rise to the Moabites and Ammonites, tribes that would become enemies of Israel.

But before you dismiss Lot, let me suggest that Lot's story is far more like ours than we may be willing to acknowledge. Oh, you won't do what he did. However, while he didn't finish well, it might surprise you how well he started. And if that is true, then we would do well to consider the temptations and choices that Lot succumbed to that led him to finish so poorly. Because those choices aren't so dissimilar to the ones we face.

Lot Starts Out With Abraham as a Pilgrim of Faith

Lot was Abraham's nephew. We meet him in the narrative when the Lord tells Abraham in Genesis 12:1-4 to leave the country he is living in and travel to a new country, one that the Lord will use to bless Abraham and his descendants.

Now the LORD said to Abram, 'Go from your country and your kindred and your father's house to the land that I will show you. And I will make of you a great nation, and I will bless you and make your name great, so that you will be a blessing. I will bless those who bless you, and him who dishonors you I will curse, and in you all the families of the earth shall be blessed.' So Abram went, as the LORD had told him, *and Lot went with him.* Abram was seventy-five years old when he departed from Haran. (Emphasis added.)

So Abraham leaves for the land God is promising and Lot goes with him. Such a significant life decision suggests Abraham has shared with Lot his encounter with God. Lot doesn't have to go. He could stay with his father Terah, Abraham's brother. But he goes, so there must have been a reason. What other reason than Abraham shared God's promise with Lot? And, as we shall see, it appears that he believed God's promise as well. He exercised faith in God too. They both journey towards a new land, a promised land. Just as we are pilgrims in this world, Abraham and Lot were too.

The Choice for Present Prosperity

However, there came a point in their journey when they had to separate. On the surface, it was a choice that made sense. But in doing so, Lot makes a choice that proves fatal for his wife and almost for himself.

On the journey, Abraham and Lot grow in wealth and it becomes clear that their herds cannot pasture together. The land simply could not support all of their livestock together. So Abraham suggests that they separate their flocks. Lot's choice is an important moment.

So Abram went up from Egypt, he and his wife and all that he had, and Lot with him, into the Negeb. Now Abram was very rich in livestock, in silver, and in gold. And he journeyed on from the Negeb as far as Bethel to the place where his tent had been at the beginning, between Bethel and Ai, to the place where he had made an altar at the first. And there Abram called upon the name of the LORD. And Lot, who went with Abram, also had flocks and herds and tents, so that the land could not support both of them dwelling together; for their possessions were so great that they could not dwell together, and there was strife between the herdsmen of Abram's livestock and the herdsmen of Lot's livestock. At that time the Canaanites and the Perizzites were dwelling in the land.

Then Abram said to Lot, 'Let there be no strife between you and me, and between your herdsmen and my herdsmen, for we are kinsmen. Is not the whole land before you? Separate yourself from me. If you take the left hand, then I will go to the right, or if you take the right hand, then I will go to the left.' And Lot lifted up his eyes and saw that the Jordan Valley was well watered everywhere like the garden of the LORD, like the land of Egypt, in the direction of Zoar. (This was before the LORD destroyed Sodom and Gomorrah.) So Lot chose for himself all the Jordan Valley, and Lot journeyed east. Abram settled in the land of Canaan, *while Lot settled among the cities of the valley and moved his tent as far as Sodom.* Now the men of Sodom were wicked, great sinners against the LORD (Gen. 13:1-13, emphasis added).

Given the choice, Lot chooses the fertile land of plenty. A land rich with potential, that could let him further increase his flocks, insuring his wealth and prosperity. Thinking about it, Lot really should have deferred to Abraham. In other words, the younger should have deferred the decision to the older. Who knows what Abraham would have chosen? Instead, while Lot could have chosen the Promised Land in Canaan, he chooses the Jordan Valley. A valley filled with cities of other tribes and people. He chooses the promise of present prosperity, rather than the promise of the future blessing.

And he travels east. Towards Sodom.

From Pilgrim to Settler to Citizen

Here is where Lot's story turns dark.

Initially, Lot simply moves down into the Jordan valley. But we find Lot somewhere different a few chapters later. Something happens over time. The world beckoned. Surely, with his flocks, he traded with the cities around him, including Sodom. He heard stories. He met traders from Sodom. He saw their prosperity. He heard about their exciting ways. He shared meals.

Despite its wickedness, he was attracted to the life of Sodom. Perhaps he was applauded and respected by the citizens there. After all, he was a prosperous man himself. Surely, he thought he would be able to resist the evil even if he lived there. He wasn't a wicked man. He had traveled with Abraham and knew the living God, at least through Abraham. Whatever the reason, we find him later in the story not just in the land but near Sodom. It wasn't a sudden thing. It took place gradually. He has gone from pilgrim to settler. And from settler to something else. He had become a citizen of Sodom.

How do we know this? When the angels come to destroy Sodom, they find Lot in Sodom.

> The two angels came to Sodom in the evening, and Lot was sitting in the gate of Sodom. When Lot saw them, he rose to meet them and bowed himself with his face to the earth and said, 'My lords, please turn aside to your servant's house and spend the night and wash your feet. Then you may rise up early and go on your way.' They said, 'No; we will spend the night in the town square.' But he pressed them strongly; so they turned aside to him and entered his house (Gen. 19: 1-3).

To sit in the gates means that you are one of the respected members in the city. Lot had changed. He was not just a shepherd outside the city. He was part of the life of Sodom. Although he knew of its immorality, instead of separating himself from it, he was being conformed to it. His home was inside the city. And it was inside that city that Lot offers his daughters to the men of Sodom to appease their lust for the angels. It was there that he hesitated in leaving. He had become someone that he likely wouldn't have recognized when he set out from Ur with Abraham.

WE ARE MORE LIKE LOT THAN WE THINK

It is easy for us to condemn Lot, but I think he represents a silent struggle that many of us face. Mind you, Lot wasn't an evil man at the outset. Abraham brought him with him when told to leave Ur by God. He knew the promises. Somewhere along the line, the lines got blurred.

We know Sodom was evil, a city of sinful lusts. But somehow, just like Lot, we can be drawn in to a culture like that. Without realizing it, we find ourselves inside Sodom.

And the seriousness of a Sodom-like culture is far greater than we think. In fact, we think that Sodom's sin was sexual immorality. But it was way worse. Listen to Ezekiel's condemnation of Sodom:

> Behold, this was the guilt of your sister Sodom: she and her daughters had pride, excess of food, and prosperous ease, but did not aid the poor and needy. They were haughty and did an abomination before me. So I removed them, when I saw it (Ezek. 16:49-50).

Tyler Kenny, digital content manager at Ligonier Ministries, makes the following observation about this passage:

> In the context surrounding this passage, Ezekiel is charging Israel for having done worse than Sodom. And what does he say was Sodom's sin? The prophet doesn't focus on any single outward behavior. Sexual immorality was an issue, as we know from Genesis, and so was her lack of concern for the poor and needy, as we see

mentioned here. But Ezekiel doesn't target either of those primarily. Rather, he says that the real issue with Sodom was her haughty heart—she was proud.

There's a warning in this for us. We must beware lest we think that the issue is simply an external one and that we are 'good with God' just because we maintain a high moral code.[1]

Again, lest we fool ourselves into thinking we couldn't possibly be like Lot, consider the warning about conformity in Psalm 1:1 (NIV):

> Blessed is the one
> who does not walk in step with the wicked
> or stand in the way that sinners take
> or sit in the company of mockers.

There is a famous progression here. First you walk with the wicked. But then you stand with them. And finally you sit in the company of mockers. Walk. Stand. Sit. Left unchecked, conformity to the world is a slow but sure progression towards a sinful lifestyle.

That's the caution in Psalm 1. You may only think that you are walking along with the wicked as you live your life. You don't identify with them. But you walk their way. You talk their way. Perhaps at work. Perhaps by what you watch on TV. Then you are standing with them. Absorbing their way of life. Then, if you aren't careful, you will find yourself sitting with them. And you won't just be sitting with them. You will be like them. Have you ever sat around with a group of people and mocked someone else? I have. It's not a proud moment. For all we think otherwise, we are one of them. Just like Lot.

---

1. Tyler Kenny, *The Sin of Sodom* (Desiring God Ministries, June 10, 2010).

THE STRONG CURRENTS OF CULTURE

Whether we wish to admit it or not, we are constantly being pressed to conform to the culture we find ourselves in. Let me share how this has worked with me, how I've been conformed. Recently, I took a look at my own life. Here's what I saw:

- Too much TV. This is an entertainment culture that we live in and I embraced it fully by watching TV.
  - o Game of Thrones
  - o Walking Dead
  - o Last Week Tonight with John Oliver
  - o Movies
  - o Sports
- Too much good living. I liked to eat good food. But how did I decide I was engaged in too much good living? I got bored if I had the same five or six different kinds of meals: Chinese, Mexican, pizza, sushi. I was living comfortably and yet, somehow, it still felt like it wasn't comfortable enough.
- I coveted things. Didn't just want them; I was unhappy that I didn't have them. I wanted the beach home. I wanted the big trips around the world. I wanted the toys.
- I counted my money like a rich man. Tracked my money daily. I thought about investments more than I did Scripture. I wanted more even though we had a lot. I worried about our financial future. Most of you are too young but, you Boomers, think Scrooge McDuck.

The result from this reflection?

- I'd become more coarse. When I was first saved, one of the miracles in my life is that I stopped swearing instantly. Before I became a Christian, I cursed all the time. But, recently, I noticed certain words creeping back into my vocabulary. I was less sensitive to coarseness.

- I'd become more self-sufficient. I prayed less. I was less prone to ask for help.
- I'd become more reliant on and trusting in my savings. Where was my treasure? See Chapter 2.
- I'd become angrier and easily annoyed. Instead of seeing people as created in the image of God, saved and unsaved, I saw people as fools. And do you know where this was most pronounced? When I was driving. Somehow, driving seems to unleash the beast in me. I'd yell at people. I'd get really angry. I would be embarrassed to be that way anywhere else. But that's what I was becoming.
- I loved my comfort. There was a certain unwillingness to sacrifice, especially my time. I had gotten to a point that I was unhappy if there was a request at church to help others.
- I loved my reputation more than the Lord. How did I know that? I was unwilling to rock the boat at work. I was a weak witness both in evangelism and in standing up for what is right biblically.

All of this doesn't happen all at once. It happened over time, just like Lot. Listen to what Watchman Nee says about Lot and us:

> Did Lot know about the conditions in Sodom? He certainly had the knowledge, for these Sodomites were quite openly wicked and exceedingly sinful against God, as the Biblical record makes plain: 'Now the men of Sodom were wicked and sinners against Jehovah exceedingly' (v.13). Yet despite his knowledge of the true state of affairs there, Lot nonetheless moved step by step in the direction of Sodom and, as we shall soon learn, eventually moved right *into* the city. As your feet draw away from other believers, your tent is bound to slowly but surely edge

closer and closer towards the Sodoms of this world. You even find yourself no longer hating what God hates and no longer condemning what God condemns as your feet gradually move farther and farther eastward.

Ironically, this is how temptation comes in. Violate your conscience a little bit today and a little bit more tomorrow; read the Bible a little less today and just a little bit less the next; pray a few minutes less today and a few minutes less tomorrow; witness a little less today and but a trifle less the next day. This is how you slide backward. Satan will not have you stop gathering, reading the Bible, praying or witnessing all at once. No, he will instead cause you to draw back little by little. He is most patient in pulling you back only gradually.[2]

All of this makes me feel that I am, uncomfortably, like Lot. And that's not how I want to finish.

THE BORDERLINE BELIEVER

Still not convinced that you could be like Lot? Perhaps you think so because you think that you are a believer and Lot wasn't. Before we decide that, let's consider history's judgment of Lot. Peter writes the following in 2 Peter 2:4-10:

> For if God did not spare angels when they sinned, but cast them into hell and committed them to chains of gloomy darkness to be kept until the judgment; if he did not spare the ancient world, but preserved Noah, a herald of righteousness, with seven others, when he brought a flood upon the world of the ungodly; if by turning the cities of Sodom and Gomorrah to ashes he condemned them to extinction, making them an example of what is going to happen to the ungodly; and if he rescued *righteous Lot*, greatly distressed by the sensual conduct of the wicked (for as that righteous man lived among them day after day, he was tormenting his righteous soul over their lawless deeds that he saw and heard); then the

---

2. Watchman Nee, *From Faith to Faith* (Christian Faith Publishers, 2014).

Lord knows how to rescue the godly from trials, and to keep the unrighteous under punishment until the day of judgment, and especially those who indulge in the lust of defiling passion and despise authority. (Emphasis added.)

Look at verse 7. Lot was not condemned by the Lord. He was declared a righteous man. Let that sink in. This is the man who moved into Sodom, who offered his daughters to the crowd, who hesitated to leave Sodom.

He was rescued by the Lord. And the Lord calls him a righteous man.

But by his choices, he succumbed to the culture, was tormented by it, and it had its impact on his life. Chris Bruno, assistant professor of New Testament and Greek at Bethlehem College and Seminary, says this:

But 2 Peter 2 confirms that Lot was indeed righteous and fills out how this righteous status affected him. He was troubled by the sin he saw around him in Sodom. However, this was not the foundation of his righteousness, but rather the result of it. Both his righteousness and ours, as 2 Peter 1:1 reminds us, is finally and fully predicated on the righteousness of our God and Savior Jesus Christ.

It seems that the only way to affirm both the account in Genesis 19 and the teaching of 2 Peter 2 is to read both in concert. And when we are reading these texts canonically and christologically, the pieces fit together in such a way that they can only lead to one conclusion: Lot was simultaneously righteous and sinful.

And more often than I'd like to admit, I act like Lot did. I am indeed troubled by the sin I see around me in the world. But far too often, I end up responding to the sin I see around me the same way that Lot did—by sinning myself. My guess is that many Christians share this experience.

But like Lot, I have also been declared righteous. Not because of what I have done, but because of what Christ has done for me. And at the end of days, I will be proclaimed righteous because I have been united to the true Righteous One. No person is proclaimed righteous apart from Christ, but all who are in him are declared righteous along with him. This is how Lot could be righteous even in the midst of his sin. So then, 2 Peter 2:7 is a testament to audaciousness of the gospel—Peter could call a man with so many obvious flaws Righteous Lot because of the promise to Abraham. And if we are in Christ, then God has rescued us as well because he remembers his promise to Abraham.[3]

As a man growing older, I would like to think I am following in the example of Caleb. Remember what Caleb said?

> And now, behold, the LORD has kept me alive, just as he said, these forty-five years since the time that the LORD spoke this word to Moses, while Israel walked in the wilderness. And now, behold, I am this day eighty-five years old. I am still as strong today as I was in the day that Moses sent me; my strength now is as my strength was then, for war and for going and coming. So now give me this hill country of which the LORD spoke on that day, for you heard on that day how the Anakim were there, with great fortified cities. It may be that the LORD will be with me, and I shall drive them out just as the LORD said (Josh. 14:10-12).

However, my fear is that I am too often more like Lot than I am like Caleb. Am I troubled by sin around me? Yes. But am I aware of how much my love of my present pleasures and my lack of a future perspective have influenced my accommodation of sin in my own life? I am not so sure about that. I love my pleasures.

Oh, may I not take the audacious gospel for granted! And may I not live like Lot in a present-day Sodom. And on the day I am buried, I pray that when some call me

---

3. Chris Bruno, 'You Asked, How Could Sinful Lot Been Righteous?' (The Gospel Coalition, February 7, 2017).

righteous in Christ, others would not think, 'Righteous? Didn't he live like the rest of us?'

TRANSFORMED, NOT CONFORMED

To find hope and a better way, let's go back to the passage at the beginning of this chapter.

> Therefore, I urge you, brothers and sisters, in view of God's mercy, to offer your bodies as a living sacrifice, holy and pleasing to God—this is your true and proper worship. Do not conform to the pattern of this world, but be transformed by the renewing of your mind. Then you will be able to test and approve what God's will is—his good, pleasing and perfect will (Rom. 12:1-2 NIV).

It is quite simple really. Either we are being transformed or conformed. There is no middle ground. We see that being conformed is the wrong way. So we need to be transformed.

How does that happen? How are our minds transformed? We know some of the answer:

- Preach the gospel to yourself daily.
- Be a committed part of a local body of believers.
- Pursue holiness.

There are wonderful books already written on those important practices. But let me suggest something else, something to help with this idea of untangling ourselves from the culture so we aren't conformed. Not try to escape to the wilderness. But untangle and then re-engage. How? By cultivating a life centered in being part of the *kingdom of God*. We don't talk a lot about the kingdom of God in normal conversations or even at church. But it is, in fact, central to everything we are and will be for eternity. We renew our minds by living as citizens of the kingdom. And by being transformed by the culture of that kingdom. A kingdom unlike any kingdom or country in this world.

Without it, we fall prey to the conforming powers of this present culture.

Russell Moore, President of the Ethics and Religious Liberty Commission of the Southern Baptist Convention, writes:

> The first question of culture is one of identity, who are we and where do we fit in the broader culture. We too often see America as somehow more 'real' than the kingdom, and our country as more important than the church.
>
> Jesus told us to seek first the kingdom of God. He taught us to pray for God's kingdom to come, on earth, as it is in heaven. The message preached both by him and the apostles was one of the kingdom that is mysteriously both here and yet to come. But the kingdom does not seem quite as real as the powers around us ... The kingdoms of the moment, whatever they are, seem more important than the kingdom of Christ, without our realizing it. That's why our blood pressure is more likely to rise when we hear someone disagree with us about our political party or our sports team or an item in the news than when we hear faulty teaching from a Christian pulpit ... The first step to a renewed vision of our mission is to see the kingdom of God in its future glory and in its present reality ... In the kingdom, we see how the gospel connects to culture and to missions. We start to be patterned toward what we should long for, what we should lament, and what justice looks like. And perhaps most importantly, in the kingdom of God, we see who we are and where we are headed. That changes both the content and the tone of our witness.[4]

In other words, there is a culture to the Kingdom of God, one that isn't rooted in this world. And we need to own it, live it and be transformed by it. Many of us know and understand the principle of putting off sinful behavior and putting on righteous behavior. This is true not only

---

4. Russell Moore, *Onward* (B&H Publishing Group, 2015), pp. 47-48.

of individual elements of holy living but of our cultural participation.

If we only practice putting off the culture of this society, without replacing it with the culture of the Kingdom of God, we can be assured that this present culture will seep back in and fill our minds and hearts again.

Clearly, Lot never had a sense of belonging to a kingdom when he entered the Jordan Valley and that made him susceptible to becoming a citizen of Sodom. Too many Christians suffer from this same sense of not belonging to a kingdom that is greater than their country of birth. When we see we are citizens of the Kingdom of God, everything changes.

In Romans 12, Paul describes what the culture of the kingdom of God looks like. Try to picture in your mind a city full of people. Countless who live like the following. This is the kingdom culture.

> Let love be genuine. Abhor what is evil; hold fast to what is good. Love one another with brotherly affection. Outdo one another in showing honor. Do not be slothful in zeal, be fervent in spirit, serve the Lord. Rejoice in hope, be patient in tribulation, be constant in prayer. Contribute to the needs of the saints and seek to show hospitality.
>
> Bless those who persecute you; bless and do not curse them. Rejoice with those who rejoice, weep with those who weep. Live in harmony with one another. Do not be haughty, but associate with the lowly. Never be wise in your own sight. Repay no one evil for evil, but give thought to do what is honorable in the sight of all. If possible, so far as it depends on you, live peaceably with all. Beloved, never avenge yourselves, but leave it to the wrath of God, for it is written, 'Vengeance is mine, I will repay, says the Lord.' To the contrary, 'if your enemy is hungry, feed him; if he is thirsty, give him something to drink; for by so doing you will heap burning coals on his head.' Do not be overcome by evil, but overcome evil with good (Rom. 12:9-21).

A more extensive description of life in the Kingdom of Heaven is contained in Jesus' Sermon on the Mount found in Matthew 5-7. Too many think it is a way of life for everyone. But the truth is that it is the way of life meant to be lived as a kingdom citizen here on earth. That is what we are being transformed into. Here's just a sample of the kind of person you and I are supposed to be:

The Beatitudes

Blessed are the poor in spirit, for theirs is the kingdom of heaven.
Blessed are those who mourn, for they shall be comforted.
Blessed are the meek, for they shall inherit the earth.
Blessed are those who hunger and thirst for righteousness, for they shall be satisfied.
Blessed are the merciful, for they shall receive mercy.
Blessed are the pure in heart, for they shall see God.
Blessed are the peacemakers, for they shall be called sons of God.
Blessed are those who are persecuted for righteousness' sake, for theirs is the kingdom of heaven.
Blessed are you when others revile you and persecute you and utter all kinds of evil against you falsely on my account. Rejoice and be glad, for your reward is great in heaven, for so they persecuted the prophets who were before you (Matt. 5:3-12).

Anger

You have heard that it was said to those of old, 'You shall not murder; and whoever murders will be liable to judgment.' But I say to you that everyone who is angry with his brother will be liable to judgment; whoever insults his brother will be liable to the council; and whoever says, 'You fool!' will be liable to the hell of fire (Matt. 5:21-22).

Lust

You have heard that it was said, 'You shall not commit adultery.' But I say to you that everyone who looks at a woman with lustful intent has already committed adultery with her in his heart (Matt. 5:27-28).

Oaths

Let what you say be simply 'Yes' or 'No'; anything more than this comes from evil (Matt. 5:37).

Retaliation

You have heard that it was said, 'An eye for an eye and a tooth for a tooth.' But I say to you, Do not resist the one who is evil. But if anyone slaps you on the right cheek, turn to him the other also (Matt. 5:38-39).

Love Your Enemies

You have heard that it was said, 'You shall love your neighbor and hate your enemy.' But I say to you, Love your enemies and pray for those who persecute you, so that you may be sons of your Father who is in heaven (Matt. 5:43-45).

Giving to the Needy

But when you give to the needy, do not let your left hand know what your right hand is doing, so that your giving may be in secret. And your Father who sees in secret will reward you (Matt. 6:3-4).

Do Not Be Anxious

Therefore I tell you, do not be anxious about your life, what you will eat or what you will drink, nor about your body, what you will put on. Is not life more than food, and the body more than clothing? ... But seek first the kingdom of God and his righteousness, and all these things will be added to you. Therefore do not be anxious about tomorrow, for tomorrow will be anxious for itself. Sufficient for the day is its own trouble (Matt. 6:25-34).

Judging Others

You hypocrite, first take the log out of your own eye, and then you will see clearly to take the speck out of your brother's eye (Matt. 7:5).

The Golden Rule

So whatever you wish that others would do to you, do also to them, for this is the Law and the Prophets (Matt. 7:12).

This is kingdom living. And it starts here in this lifetime. We aren't simply putting off an old lifestyle of sin. It's a legalistic fallacy to think of sanctification that way. Do this. Don't do that. It's the wrong starting point and the wrong understanding of a transforming work that began the minute you were saved. We are acclimatizing ourselves to our new citizenship and nature. And the more we live as citizens of such a kingdom, the more likely we are to finish well.

CONCLUSION

As we grow older, I think the temptation is to settle for what we've become. We did the best we could, now we are what we are. But that is not biblical thinking. The transformation isn't supposed to end until the day we die.

Let's not choose Lot's way. Let's not end with lives tormented by the lawlessness of this world, living as those who have deceived themselves into being conformed by this culture without realizing it. Let's test what we believe and enjoy and hold onto and how we live. And let's be transformed by the renewing of our mind.

Let's be found more and more to be the Kingdom citizens that we are—engaged with the world but transformed as citizens with our eyes on the King and the life to come.

How do we fight the temptation to conform to the world in the last season of our lives? We keep pruning the branches of our lives. Just like in a vineyard. When I buy wine, I often read how the best wine is from the oldest branches. But to be producing branches, they have to be pruned over a lifetime. If you give up pruning, they become wild and unproductive.

That pruning in our lives is continuing to cut away the sins and heart attitudes that rob us of our sweet life in Christ. And more, it is embracing the life in Christ. Embracing humility over pride. Embracing grace towards others over anger. Embracing generosity over selfishness. Embracing kindness over cruelty and gossip. And remember, it's an arc. It doesn't happen all at once. It takes a lifetime. And even then, the best is yet to come.

To do that, let me close with this. I don't think we do it alone, especially in this age. Russell Moore writes,

> For Christians, our consciences and thought patterns are formed together, by life together in the community of the kingdom. There are so many ways that cultural norms seduce us, we have to find local communities of believers and live out life with them. Perhaps you have had bad experiences with churches. Ok. But the call remains, don't forsake the local gathering. Find good, bible believing churches that are practicing, as best they can, what it means to be a local expression of the body of Christ to the glory of God, practicing true fellowship, sharing the gospel and being as authentic as they can. They won't be perfect but, then, you aren't either.[5]

Finishing well isn't supposed to be a solitary effort. You are being prepared to live in heaven. Start to live that kingdom life here on earth now.

5.. Russell Moore, *ibid*, p. 84.

5

Paul, Burroughs and Christian Contentment

in Spite of our Prosperity

An ornate, calligraphic letter in a word adds no more meaning to the word than any other letter; neither does the fancy material thing make a man better for it. (Jeremiah Burroughs)

INTRODUCTION

The messages at the beach were always tailored for a particular group: those growing older, with children grown or almost grown. We've had long experiences as believers and in the church. We were all leaders or former leaders. And most of us were prosperous materially. Not wealthy by worldly standards. But prosperous.

And some of you are like that. You have high incomes. You have abundant possessions. You have investments. Spacious homes. New or newer cars. Plenty of food and clothes. Maybe you eat out a lot. Maybe you go on lots of trips and vacations. You may have a vacation home or rentals. Large 401(k) annuities. Or expensive leisure pursuits. If that's you, I think that this season of life presents a very big challenge for you. And even if you aren't as prosperous, living in the

119

United States presents a temptation to covet prosperity as if it were the key to happiness and contentment.

The irony about living in the United States is that it seems that fewer and fewer people are living contented lives, despite their wealth and prosperity. We are so busy with work and family, so preoccupied with our lives, so overwhelmed with social media, so distracted by sports and leisure and movies and music, so distracted by food, alcohol and drugs, that we find it hard to live contentedly. Furthermore, the country is seemingly more and more divided with hot passions among various groups of people. There is political stress, economic stress, racial stress, health stress, international stress, ethnic stress, class stress, educational stress. And then there are all the anxieties that so many of us face. Consider the rampant opioid scourge in the country, environmental concerns, and psychological stressors from bullying to sexual harassment. How can such a wealthy nation find itself so subject to such mental and emotional stress and anxiety? Shouldn't we be the happiest, most contented of all people when we are such a wealthy nation?

What is our frame of mind as we live prosperously? What shapes our attitudes, our reactions to situations, our view of others? This message is about learning the secret to living a contented life in the midst of prosperity.

WHAT IS BIBLICAL CONTENTMENT?

Let's start with a biblical passage.

> Rejoice in the Lord always; again I will say, rejoice. Let your reasonableness be known to everyone. The Lord is at hand; do not be anxious about anything, but in everything by prayer and supplication with thanksgiving let your requests be made known to God. And the peace of God, which surpasses all understanding, will guard your hearts and your minds in Christ Jesus.

Finally, brothers, whatever is true, whatever is honorable, whatever is just, whatever is pure, whatever is lovely, whatever is commendable, if there is any excellence, if there is anything worthy of praise, think about these things. What you have learned and received and heard and seen in me—practice these things, and the God of peace will be with you.

I rejoiced in the Lord greatly that now at length you have revived your concern for me. You were indeed concerned for me, but you had no opportunity. Not that I am speaking of being in need, for *I have learned in whatever situation I am to be content.* I know how to be brought low, and I know how to abound. In any and every circumstance, I have learned the secret of facing plenty and hunger, abundance and need. I can do all things through him who strengthens me. (Phil. 4:4-13, emphasis added).

Contentment has the connotation that one is satisfied and restful and happy. But Christian contentment is more specific.

Thomas Watson in *The Devine Art of Contentment* defines it as 'a sweet temper of spirit, whereby a Christian *carries himself in equal poise* in every condition.'[1] (Emphasis added.)

Jeremiah Burroughs in *The Rare Jewel of Christian Contentment* defines it as 'that sweet, inward, quiet, gracious frame of spirit, which freely submits to and delights in God's wise and fatherly disposal in every condition.'[2]

From this, we can conclude that Christian contentment is not a state of being such as:

---

1. Thomas Watson, *The Devine Art of Contentment* (Soli Deo Publications, Reprint taken from the 1835 edition), p. 31.

2. Jeremiah Burroughs, *The Rare Jewel of Christian Contentment* (Banner of Truth Trust, reprinted 1995), p. 40.

- A sporadic, occasional feeling based on external conditions. Believers and unbelievers alike can be content after eating a meal or for a brief moment after Christmas.
- The Greek Stoic notion of contentment, which was a human-based sense of endurance through all human experience.

Christian contentment, then, is:
- Inward—From our soul, irrespective of external conditions.
- Divine—Originating in God. It is a work of the Spirit.

Christian contentment is that inward sense of peace and calm and satisfaction, resting and trusting in the loving care of our sovereign Father, regardless of the material and psychological conditions we find ourselves in. It anchors our emotions to a secure and quiet joyful sense that we are ok, are going to be ok and can look forward to God bringing us home to Him.

It is important to point out that Christian contentment isn't the absence of pressures or trouble or challenges in our lives. It isn't the absence of storms, suffering or sorrow in our life. It's not some kind of phony feel-good emotionalism. It isn't a positive mental attitude that ignores reality. Rather, it is the calm in the midst of such seasons of life. In fact, Christian contentment only works as we live in the midst of our realities.

A pastor once suggested a response to the question, 'How are you?' that captures a contented soul. Most people simply treat it an informal greeting. The answer he gave? 'Doing better than I deserve.' The contented Christian knows that he or she is the recipient of amazing grace in salvation, which is our greatest need. Further, he or she knows that God is working everything for our good, whether that comes in the form or blessing or trial. And he or she knows that the Lord will not only hold us close in this life but will bring us home to Him in death. These truths push anxiety to the fringes. If contentment is the opposite of worry and anxiety, then Christian contentment is the banishment of anxiety and replacing it with a settled, joyful sense of trust and peace regardless of your circumstances, as troubling or concerning as they might be.

Let me give an example. I related in Chapter 2 how badly I reacted when I stepped down as a pastor and the sinful fear I gave in to about my financial security. However, years later, when I lost my job because the company lost its contract, the temptation was to worry, to stress, and certainly not to be at peace. But rather than be consumed with all the anxieties that come from being out of work, I trusted in the Lord. It doesn't mean that there weren't real issues to deal with—finding another job, figuring out a new budget, dealing with the fact that employers don't really want older, new employees, etc. And that relationship with the Lord was the source of my contentment. I was content before I lost my job. I was content after I lost my job. Did I want another job? Of course! However, my contentment wasn't grounded in my circumstances; it was grounded in God my Father. He is sovereign. He loves me. My worth isn't bound up in what I do. And my security, my true security, is grounded in the Lord I love and serve.

Finally, the contentment that Paul writes about is something different from worldly contentment. Worldly contentment says make yourself safe, make yourself prosperous, make yourself healthy, make yourself beautiful and you will be content. That's not Christian contentment. It is a secret. The contentment Paul writes of is not apparent to the unbeliever. People are looking for contentment in all the wrong places. This secret contentment has to be revealed by the Lord. Notice that Paul says that this contentment is a secret he has learned. As Christians, contentment is something that must be uncovered by the Lord, then understood, and then practiced.

One of my favorite hymns speaks about contentment in real life, 'Blessed Be Your Name,' by Matt Redman. It recognizes the wide swath our lives take, from prosperity to dark times. But we can still bless His name because we know who He is and who we are.

Blessed Be Your name
In the land that is plentiful
Where Your streams of abundance flow
Blessed be Your name.

Blessed Be Your name
When I'm found in the desert place
Though I walk through the wilderness
Blessed Be Your name.

...

Blessed be Your name
On the road marked with suffering
Though there's pain in the offering
Blessed be Your name.

Every blessing You pour out I'll
Turn back to praise
When the darkness closes in, Lord
Still I will say:

Blessed be the name of the Lord...
Blessed be your Glorious name.

I encourage you to take the time to play the song.

Since it is something to be learned, many Christians go through life not knowing the secret of Christian contentment and they live their lives much as unbelievers do, overly affected by external circumstances and basing the peace in their life on outward, not inward, factors.

THE IRONY–CHRISTIAN CONTENTMENT IS HARD TO LEARN *IN THE MIDST OF PROSPERITY*

And now we come to the main point of this chapter. Notice Paul's references to contentment in prosperity.

Paul says he has learned to be content: 'for I have learned in whatever situation I am to be content. I know how to be brought low, and I know *how to abound*. In any and every circumstance, I have learned the secret of facing *plenty* and hunger, *abundance* and need.' (Emphasis added.)

If I look at when I have experienced the peace and contentment of God most significantly, I have to admit that it comes more often during difficult times. Because difficult times, hard times, suffering, often strip away the other reasons for being content and make us more dependent on God, pointing us more to Him.

I think that Christian contentment is actually harder to gain in prosperity than in poverty and hardship. When things are going well, when we are experiencing the blessing of prosperity, then contentment, Christian contentment, becomes harder to live in. Here are some reasons why:

- Prosperous people have more responsibilities and thus more worries.
- They have more time for relaxation and entertainment and thus more temptations to love the world.
- They have more possessions to be concerned with and make idols of. In other words, possessions become the source of their happiness and contentment.
- They have the means to have more and the temptation to want more.

- They have been successful and tend to rely more on the means to that success rather than rely on the Lord.
- They have the ability to know about the world and are caught up in the cares of the world.
- They are more susceptible to humanistic theories and philosophies and religious thoughts. Other ways of thought explain human behavior. None of which lead you into godly contentment because their premises are wrong.

What I've realized over time is that the 'contentment' I experienced in my prosperity was not a biblical or Christian contentment. Oh, I am grateful for my prosperity. But I often confuse self-sufficiency and insulation from adversity and the abundance of my current circumstances with my sense of peace and satisfaction in Christ. I wouldn't say it out loud but I am really thinking, 'I am content because I am prosperous. Thank you for that, Lord.'

And if you are prosperous, then finishing well means mastering contentment in prosperity. Otherwise, the cares and burdens and temptations of this world will create a false foundation of contentment that will evaporate in times of hardship, illness and impending death.

MANAGING CONTENTMENT IN OUR PROSPERITY

What Paul suggests in Philippians is that Christ-centered contentment is not dependent on being poor or rich. It comes from the Lord and is an inward work in our heart that flows out to our lives.

Fortunately, there is good guidance on how to tend to our contentment in the season of prosperity. What follows is guidance from a dear book, *Contentment, Prosperity, and God's Glory*, by Jeremiah Burroughs. He is known by some from his classic *The Rare Jewel of Christian Contentment*.

He wrote this book after the Rare Jewel and did it because he felt that rich Christians needed more instruction on godly contentment than people who were suffering.

Burroughs knew what he was writing about. He knew what it was to be poor, to be persecuted and suffer and how to live in prosperity. He was born in England in 1599 and entered the ministry in 1625. After preaching in various churches, he became the pastor of a church with a small congregation in 1631. His income in those days was very small. Then he was suspended from ministry in 1636 during the persecution of Puritan Christians known as non-conformists. (They refused to abide by rules set by the Church of England that they felt went against Scripture.) Ultimately, he was forced to leave England for Holland in 1638. He returned to England in 1641 and became the pastor teacher of three churches, two of which were large, prominent and wealthy. He even preached in Parliament several times. It was in these later years that he wrote *The Rare Jewel of Christian Contentment*. However, it was while pastoring these rich churches and making a good income that he realized that Christian contentment was particularly challenging for the prosperous Christian. And so this book was written originally as an appendix to *Rare Jewel* and posthumously published as its own book entitled *Four Useful Discourses*. (He died in 1646 as a result of a fall from a horse.)

The remainder of this chapter now draws from *Contentment, Prosperity, and God's* Glory, which stands as its own important contribution to finishing well.

As a good Puritan who loves to parse and parse and parse, Burroughs has approximately fifty points to growing in contentment in your prosperity. (Seriously, these Puritans sliced and diced everything they thought about in ways we don't today!) Feel free to read the book but here let me relate a few points with my own interjections.

1. Biblical contentment is rooted in knowing the source

*from where all our good comes, knowing the Fountain
from where all his good springs.* [3]

The danger a prosperous man or woman faces is forgetting the source of his or her prosperity. He or she begins to forget that everything is from God's hand. He is the source. Not our hard work. Not our inheritance. Not our investments. Knowing this and reminding ourselves prevents us from making an idol out of our prosperity.

Here is an interesting Biblical passage by Job:

> And he said, 'Naked I came from my mother's womb, and naked shall I return. The LORD gave, and the LORD has taken away; blessed be the name of the LORD' (Job 1:21).

Job's story is well known. He was a prosperous man who faithfully worshipped God when Satan asks God to test Job's faith. God permits it and Job loses all but his wife. Wealth and children are taken from him with no explanation. He is afflicted with a lasting, painful sickness. For Job to make this statement, that the Lord takes away, he first had to know that the Lord was the One who gave him all his riches. Is that something we do? Remind ourselves that all that we have, all of our possessions, are from the Lord? Not just as head knowledge, but in heartfelt gratitude? And can we say with Job if we lose what we have, 'Blessed be the name of the Lord'?

2. Contentment is proportional to our awareness of our dependence on God in the height of our prosperity as we are in the depth of our adversity. [4]

Burroughs writes, 'Even noblemen and princes, if Christ has taught them this lesson, will come daily to God's grace in prayer to beg for their daily bread.' [5]

3. Jeremiah Burroughs, *Contentment, Prosperity, and God's Glory* (Reform Heritage Books, 2013), p. 93.

4. Burroughs, *Ibid*, p. 92.

5. Burroughs, *Ibid*, p. 92.

The Lord's Prayer is not for the poor only. 'Give us this day our daily bread.' Whether said by a poor man or a rich man, the right thinking is that God is the One who provides for us daily. We are completely dependent on Him. Even if you have a million dollars in the bank, contentment is obtained when you still come to the Lord each day for your daily provision.

3. Contentment is anchored by regularly surrendering up our estate, our comforts, and our possessions to God.[6]

It is one thing to know that all that we have is from the Lord. It is another thing to 'give it back' in a sense.

In prayer, we regularly acknowledge that all that we have belongs to God. It always has. It always will. This kind of prayer includes this idea from Burroughs: 'It all belongs to Thee and I desire to enjoy it no further than is needed for me to be useful to Thee ... I surrender myself and all my usefulness to Thee. Take it all. It is at Thy disposal.'[7]

But it is when we actually loosen our grip on our wealth and possessions that true Christian contentment is possible. And doing so is possible only if we are genuinely content in the Lord.

4. The Christian learns how to be [content] in this mysterious way: he learns how to have comfort in his riches by putting his affections for those riches to death.[8]

It sounds like a paradox but there is a truth to it.

---

6. Burroughs, *Ibid*, pp. 76-77.

7. Burroughs, *Ibid*, p. 77.

8. Burroughs, *Ibid*, p. 80.

A godly man moderates his spirit in the joy he receives from what God has given him; in that way he receives greater joy from them.[9]

In other words, by continually attending to our natural desire to love what we have more than we love the Lord, by keeping our affections for our riches under control, the more comfort we have in the midst of His abundance.

This is both a spiritual and practical exercise. If you have great wealth, you shouldn't ignore it. But as you take inventory, practice reminding yourself who it is from, who it really belongs to. A friend once had his car totaled in an accident by someone else. Rather than being angry, he made the following statement, 'Well, it was God's car.' And in doing so, he experienced a contentment that most people would not be able to lay hold of.

5. *The godly man understands the vanity of created things, as well as their uncertainty.*[10]

Here is a valuable quote from Burroughs in assessing the importance of what we own: 'An ornate, calligraphic letter in a word adds no more meaning to the word than any other letter; neither does the fancy material thing make a man better for it.'[11] And, 'What are these things compared to an immortal soul? They don't make me different from others who don't have such things.'[12]

Consider what Paul says about riches in 1 Timothy:

> As for the rich in this present age, charge them not to be haughty, *nor to set their hopes on the uncertainty of riches,* but on God, who richly provides us with everything to enjoy (1 Tim. 6:17, emphasis added).

---

9. Burroughs, *Ibid*, p. 80.

10. Burroughs, *Ibid*, p. 96.

11. Burroughs, *Ibid*, p. 16.

12. Burroughs, *Ibid*, p. 96.

It is so tempting to think more highly of yourself, to think yourself as somehow a better person because of your prosperity. Most of us would never say so outright, but inwardly, as we drive our cars, go on our vacations, wear our clothes, play our video games, call on our latest phones, we secretly think that somehow we are better people for it all.

And both Paul and Burroughs remind us of the foolishness of such thinking:

> Our homes are richly furnished but how quickly God may bring a fire...Even if God lets us keep our wealth, what if he alters our health so we cannot enjoy it?[13]

> Let God touch me in my brain, and I will not know how to make use of my estate.[14] (In other words, if we were to lose our minds, our wealth would be meaningless to us.)

Solomon came to understand the vanity of wealth. Listen to his conclusion about gaining such wealth in Ecclesiastes 2:

> I said in my heart, 'Come now, I will test you with pleasure; enjoy yourself.' But behold, this also was vanity. I said of laughter, 'It is mad,' and of pleasure, 'What use is it?' I searched with my heart how to cheer my body with wine—my heart still guiding me with wisdom—and how to lay hold on folly, till I might see what was good for the children of man to do under heaven during the few days of their life. I made great works. I built houses and planted vineyards for myself. I made myself gardens and parks, and planted in them all kinds of fruit trees. I made myself pools from which to water the forest of growing trees. I bought male and female slaves, and had slaves who were born in my house. I had also great possessions of herds and flocks, more than any who had been before me in Jerusalem. I also gathered for myself silver and gold and the treasure of kings and provinces. I got singers,

---

13. Burroughs, *Ibid*, pp. 96-97.

14. Burroughs, *Ibid*, p. 97.

both men and women, and many concubines, the delight of the sons of man.

So I became great and surpassed all who were before me in Jerusalem. Also my wisdom remained with me. And whatever my eyes desired I did not keep from them. I kept my heart from no pleasure, for my heart found pleasure in all my toil, and this was my reward for all my toil. *Then I considered all that my hands had done and the toil I had expended in doing it, and behold, all was vanity and a striving after wind, and there was nothing to be gained under the sun* (Eccles. 2:1-11, emphasis added).

Contentment isn't found in the abundance of possessions. While we can enjoy the blessings of prosperity, we must never give them such value or permanence that our lives and contentment depend on them.

6. *The believer learns how to be [content] in this mysterious way: he seeks to preserve his comforts and enrich himself by sharing what he has.*[15]

Hence 1 Tim 6:17-18 says:

As for the rich in this present age, charge them not to be haughty, nor to set their hopes on the uncertainty of riches, but on God, who richly provides us with everything to enjoy. They are to do good, to be rich in good works, to be generous and ready to share.

The contented man does not try to hold on to what God has given him; rather, he shares what has been given by God's grace.

If it is hard to share freely and liberally, if you think it is better to be frugal with wealth than generous, then you have to ask yourself if your prosperity is the foundation of your contentment.

I've found great joy in being able to bless others out of my abundance. But I've also noticed a certain dying when

15. Burroughs, *Ibid*, p. 78.

I do so. That love of what I have loosens its grip ever so slightly each time. It's like taking an ax to a tree. The tree doesn't fall in one blow. But each time you strike the tree with an ax, the tree shakes. And then, blow after blow, the tree can no longer stay upright. Generosity with our wealth is like that. It strikes death blow after death blow to our love of money, love of treasure, greed and selfishness.

Resolve to be rich in good works. Resolve to be generous in this lifetime. And discover how much more contented your life is. The idea of 'pay it forward' becomes a gospel principle.

7. The Christian grows in contentment by sanctifying all he has by the Word and prayer.[16]

Burroughs writes:

> If a man appreciates what he has through the lens of the Word of the promise or by the Word of the gospel, his ability to profit from the things he enjoys becomes transformed by Jesus Christ, who sanctifies everything in us.[17]

For that reason, Burroughs argues that those who are rich in this world must be familiar with the Scriptures: 'Those of us who are prosperous have more need to know the Scriptures and be in the Scriptures.'[18]

Likewise, prayer rightly sanctifies and sets apart our abundance.

> When I receive any good from any created thing then I am to seek God in prayer, that I may have a sanctified use of it. A godly man never prays more than when God prospers him in this world ... The more any man has, the

---

16. Burroughs, *Ibid*, p. 83.

17. Burroughs, *Ibid*, p. 85.

18. Burroughs, *Ibid*, p. 86.

PRESSING ON, FINISHING WELL

more need he has to pray; therefore, rich men need to pray more than poor men.[19]

Besides instructing us on the deceitfulness of wealth and the source of wealth, the Scriptures and prayer are a means of grace to us about our wealth. How often I forget who I am, where my prosperity really comes from, where my contentment lies. When I turn the Scripture, when I pray, the truth of my situation comes back like a strong wind blowing away the fog in my mind and heart.

8. A godly man increases in humility as his prosperity increases.[20]

Burroughs sees this truth, 'to see a man humbled by his prosperity is rare indeed.'[21]

In 2 Samuel 7, God tells David of the great wealth that is going to be his. David's response is not to consider how great he is to become. Rather, he asks, 'Who am I?' and 'What is my house?' David, the great man of God, the great king, recognizes that he is nothing compared to the greatness of God.

Burroughs encourages us to pray in a similar manner, and with frequency:

> Oh this is a sign of true humility, when you find your income to be more than it had been previously and then to get alone and sit before the Lord ... fall down, humble your soul, saying, 'Oh Lord, who am I, that Thou should deal so graciously with me and that Thou should make such a difference between me and others?'[22]

Consider how you are with your wealth. Are you genuinely humble? I know a man in my church who is quite well off.

19. Burroughs, *Ibid*, p. 86.

20. Burroughs, *Ibid*, p. 87.

21. Burroughs, *Ibid*, p. 87.

22. Burroughs, *Ibid*, p. 89.

But you wouldn't know it by how he conducts himself. He is generous. And more than that, he is a humble servant. He doesn't trumpet his wealth. He treats others as his equals. He serves in the simplest ways. He gets it about wealth. It doesn't make him a better man. He knows he was made in the image of God long before he became rich. And he was saved not because of his wealth but because he was a sinner, a rebel, whose sins were forgiven, whose righteousness could not be bought.

It is a great blessing to be prosperous. And rightly grasped—who it is from and how it compares to the greatness of God—it is something that should humble us. When it does, contentment follows.

9. *A godly man learns the lesson of the fear of God with respect to his prosperity.*[23]

Consider this biblical reminder to Israel about who delivered them and who prospered them:

> Hear therefore, O Israel, and be careful to do them, that it may go well with you, and that you may multiply greatly, as the LORD, the God of your fathers, has promised you, in a land flowing with milk and honey. Hear, O Israel: The LORD our God, the LORD is one. You shall love the LORD your God with all your heart and with all your soul and with all your might. ... And when the LORD your God brings you into the land that he swore to your fathers, to Abraham, to Isaac, and to Jacob, to give you—with great and good cities that you did not build, and houses full of all good things that you did not fill, and cisterns that you did not dig, and vineyards and olive trees that you did not plant—and when you eat and are full, *then take care lest you forget the LORD, who brought you out of the land of Egypt, out of the house of slavery* (Deut. 6:3-12, emphasis added).

---

23. Burroughs, *Ibid*, p. 94.

It is an instructive passage. Like Israel, we have been delivered out of the land of slavery, our own sinfulness, into a land of milk and honey. While the land of milk and honey for us is the kingdom of heaven, in a secondary sense, we do live in a land of milk and honey in terms of our prosperity.

And the warning? Fear God. Do not forget Him who delivered you into such prosperity.

10. The godly man learns the excellence and value of true riches, namely spiritual riches.[24]

Burroughs reports that Martin Luther used to say, 'The smallest degree of grace, and every gracious work, is worth more than heaven and earth.'[25] Burroughs adds, 'He (Luther) professed that he would rather understand one psalm than to have all the riches of the world.'[26]

It's one thing to realize that our material prosperity is not our true treasure; but what do we actively value in its place? Martin Luther would count understanding a single psalm above all the riches in the world. Honestly, I am not there yet. As much as I love the Scriptures, the love of money and wealth still tugs at my heart.

What are some of our true riches? Here is one inventory:

- Our salvation in Christ.
- Our justification in which our sins are imputed to Christ and His righteousness is imputed to us.
- The forgiveness of our sins. Our adoption as children of the Father.
- Being born again as a new creation.
- Being in union with Christ.

---

24. Burroughs, *Ibid*, p. 99.

25. Burroughs, *Ibid*, p. 99.

26. Burroughs, *Ibid*, p. 99.

- The promise of an inheritance that will never fade nor perish. Being part of a community of believers in the true church.

- Being empowered by His Spirit for holy living.

Our greatest treasure of all? Knowing Jesus. Being in fellowship with Him. The experience of being loved by Him. As Paul writes, we are in a relationship in which we increasingly 'comprehend the breadth and length and height and depth, and to know the love of Christ that surpasses knowledge, that you may be filled with all the fullness of God.' A content man or woman has learned this lesson. Not just in the general knowing but in the daily reality of our hearts.

11. *The contented man knows that God sets this time in his life as the time to provide for eternity.*[27]

Ironically, many prosperous people understand the nature of financial investment but not so much the nature of investing for eternity. We invest wealth now, with the anticipation that later we may have a greater abundance. But we somehow forget that the same is true with eternity. How we live now is our investment in our eternal life to come.

The parable of the talents teaches us that. In Matthew 25, Jesus tells the story of a man who goes on a journey. He entrusts three of his servants with some of his wealth while he is gone. One servant receives one talent; the second servant receives two talents; the third is given five talents. When the master returns, he summons the servants to settle the accounts. Two of them return what was entrusted to them with more, having increased the wealth they had been given. To them, the master commends their efforts on his behalf:

---

27. Burroughs, *Ibid*, p. 100.

> His master said to him, 'Well done, good and faithful servant. You have been faithful over a little; I will set you over much. Enter into the joy of your master' (Matt. 25:21).

And

> His master said to him, 'Well done, good and faithful servant. You have been faithful over a little; I will set you over much. Enter into the joy of your master' (Matt. 25:23).

But one returned only what he had received, explaining that he had been afraid of the master and hoarded what he had been given. The master's judgment is severe:

> But his master answered him, 'You wicked and slothful servant! You knew that I reap where I have not sown and gather where I scattered no seed? Then you ought to have invested my money with the bankers, and at my coming I should have received what was my own with interest. So take the talent from him and give it to him who has the ten talents' (Matt. 25:26-28).

Then the master lays out the principle that all of us with wealth should hear as a principle of the life to come:

> For to everyone who has will more be given, and he will have an abundance. But from the one who has not, even what he has will be taken away. And cast the worthless servant into the outer darkness. In that place there will be weeping and gnashing of teeth (Matt. 25:29-30).

Our prosperity isn't meant so much to be enjoyed now but to be used as an investment for the eternal life to come. What we do with our gifts and talents and even our riches, all of which come from the Lord, will have an effect on our eternal life. We don't really know what that means. However, it is clear that being prosperous in this lifetime and how we live in that prosperity sets the stage for our lives in heaven.

Put another way, do we want to hear, 'Well done, good and faithful servant. You have been faithful over a little; I will set you over much. Enter into the joy of your master.'? Christian contentment is a key to living prosperously to the glory of God because we refuse to let prosperity be an end in itself and the source of our contentment. Instead, we are content with our lives, regardless of our prosperity, for we have the reality of Jesus now and for eternity in view.

WHAT CHOKES GODLY CONTENTMENT?

There are some behaviors that should warn us that we aren't really walking in contentment in our prosperity. And they take the power out of our contentment. Here are several that Burroughs identifies. And they are as likely to strike us in our prosperity as in our want.

1. Having a murmuring and complaining heart. While complaining is a universal human trait not just limited to the prosperous, prosperity gives us more time to complain. Plus, we are more invested in this world and are more likely to complain and murmur.

2. Having a tumultuous mind. Burroughs explains it as 'when thoughts run distractingly and work in a confused manner, so that the affections (your feelings) are like an unruly multitude.' Isn't this so true in our age when we are bombarded by so many sources that demand our attention! The prosperous can be even more full of distracted thinking because we have more, we are responsible for more, we feel more pressure to manage and even because there is more to enjoy.

    Take time to be quiet and do nothing rashly. Disengage from social media. Turn off the TV. Close your laptops. Be still and know that God is God. Let your mind be controlled in its thinking.

3. Having distracting, heart-consuming cares. Take care not to allow fear and the distraction of bad news to take such a hold on your heart as to allow it to struggle inwardly. Burroughs notes:

> A great man will permit common people to stand outside his doors, but he will not let them come in and make a noise in his closet or bedroom when he deliberately retires from worldly business. So a well-tempered spirit may inquire after things outside in the world, and suffer some ordinary cares and fears to break into the suburbs of the soul, as to touch lightly on the thoughts. Yet it will not on any account allow an intrusion into the private room, which should be wholly reserved for Jesus Christ as his outward temple.[28]

The contented soul allows our innermost union with Christ to settle our hearts. Then that contentment extends outwardly to all circumstances, including the great concerns that afflict us, be they finances, family, or life's cares and worries that press us.

4. Being subject to sinking discouragements. Discouragement is the enemy of contentment. It opens the door to anxiety, fear, and a letting go of the truth of God's love for us. It grabs us and pulls us down into a downward cycle of condemnation, hopelessness and disappointment.

    Consider what Burroughs says about this:

> When things do not fall out according to expectation, when the tide of second causes runs so low that we see little in outward means to support our hopes and hearts. God would have us to depend on him though we do not see how the thing may be

---

28. Jeremiah Burroughs, *The Rare Jewel of Christian Contentment* (Banner of Truth Trust, 1995), p. 23.

brought about; otherwise, we do not show a quiet spirit.[29]

CONCLUSION

As prosperous Christians, we have a greater blessing in a certain way but also a greater responsibility. Prosperity handled well can be a source of great blessing. Lived well, our prosperity offers the opportunity to be a generous people. But we also have a greater source of temptation. Prosperity can also either seduce us away from the love of God with pleasure or it can distract us from that love with anxiety about having so much.

The secret of contentment will keep us from great regrets about our prosperity:

- It will keep us close to the Lord.
- It will teach us how to use our prosperity to advance His kingdom.
- It will teach us to look to eternity.
- It even teaches us how to enjoy the blessings we have without guilt.

What does your heart tell you as you get older? Are you becoming more content? If not, why not? Have you lost sight of your great treasure in Christ? Are you consumed with worries and cares in this world? Are you beset by worry or grief or regret or terror? Jesus offers you a way out of those burdens and anxieties. Come unto me, He says, and He will give you rest.

If you are more content, don't just stop there. What is the foundation of your contentment? If it is anything other than Jesus, can you sense that your life is built on a faulty foundation? Does it matter to you that Jesus is not the foundation for your life? Don't just make room for Jesus. As I write this chapter, it is almost Christmas. A popular

---

29. Burroughs, *Ibid*, p. 22-23.

Christmas carol is 'Joy to the World.' The first verse goes like this:

Joy to the world! The Lord is come!
Let earth receive her King ;
Let every heart prepare Him room,
And heaven and nature sing,
And heaven and nature sing,
And heaven, and heaven, and nature sing.

I want to suggest something heretical in terms of this beloved song. The song gets it wrong when it says, 'Let every heart prepare Him room.' I understand that it is suggesting we invite Jesus into our lives. But it gets it wrong in this way: We don't just make some room for Jesus. To do so simply puts Him someplace in the house with everything else. It's easy to lose things in a cluttered house. And if you just make room for Him in your life, I promise you, you will lose Jesus, maybe not forever but too often to live contentedly. Salvation doesn't make room for Jesus. Salvation involves a wholesale move. We move into a house that Jesus is building. We don't make room for Jesus. He makes room for us. He makes a new life for us to occupy and live in.

God gave Caleb his promised land to take ownership of. Similarly, we have been given an entirely new life by Jesus. And we are taking ownership of it, day by day. Sometimes there is struggle (well, ok, a lot of the time.) Sometimes there is suffering. But it's a whole new life. When we get that, it is way harder to lose our treasure. And much easier to learn the secret of contentment. And on that great day when we die, we won't be like the servant who buried his talent. We won't be like Solomon whose love of foreign women drew him away from the Lord. We won't be like Lot who was conformed to the love of this world. We will be like Paul who was content even when facing his own imminent execution.

6

Finishing Well
the Demas Caution

You may love worldly things—but they cannot love you in return. You love gold and silver—but your gold cannot love you in return. You give away your love to the creature—and receive no love back. But if you love God, He will love you in return. 'If any man loves me, my Father will love him, and we will come unto him, and make our abode with him' (John 14:23). God will not be behind in love to us. For our *drop* of love to Him—we shall receive an *ocean!* (Thomas Watson)

INTRODUCTION

Finishing well inevitably includes watching others not finishing well. I can name far too many who started out well as Christians but are now pursuing a different life, who don't treasure Jesus or who deny Him outright. I am not angry at them. I think, 'There, but for the grace of God, go I.' What I am, is sad. I miss them. I am sad that they left the faith. And I am sad at what they will encounter when they come face to face with the Savior they walked away from.

Despite the sorrow their lives evoke in us, their lives offer lessons for us: what not to do. How to avoid that same path. The Bible has its own list. In this chapter, we will learn the warning tale about an obscure figure from the Bible. Although he is obscure, his failure to follow Jesus is frighteningly contemporary.

This is a story about Demas. Although he is barely known to us and only mentioned a few times in the New Testament, he was closely associated with Paul; in fact, he traveled personally with Paul and Luke. Demas was a person of note in his own way.

We read about him in the book of Philemon when Paul greets the church:

> Epaphras, my fellow prisoner in Christ Jesus, sends greetings to you, and so do Mark, Aristarchus, *Demas*, and Luke, my fellow workers (Philem. 24:23-24, emphasis added).

This would have been about A.D. 62, when Paul was under house arrest in Rome. Demas is with Paul, Mark and Luke, great leaders of the early church. And it is clear that he is a part of the inner circle. In fact, we read about him again in Colossians. Commentators also date this book to Paul's first arrest.

> Aristarchus my fellow prisoner greets you, and Mark the cousin of Barnabas (concerning whom you have received instructions—if he comes to you, welcome him), and Jesus who is called Justus. These are the only men of the circumcision among my fellow workers for the kingdom of God, and they have been a comfort to me. Epaphras, who is one of you, a servant of Christ Jesus, greets you, always struggling on your behalf in his prayers, that you may stand mature and fully assured in all the will of God. For I bear him witness that he has worked hard for you and for those in Laodicea and in Hierapolis. Luke the beloved physician greets you, *as does Demas* (Col. 4: 10-14, emphasis added).

That arrest ended with Paul's release and Paul apparently conducted another missionary trip that was not recorded in Acts. Some speculate that Paul traveled to Spain and perhaps even to England. Does Demas continue to travel with Paul? Does he stay in Rome to encourage the church there? We don't know. Demas will be mentioned only one more time.

Paul was arrested again in Rome and was martyred in A.D. 67 or 68. The second arrest was more severe. It wasn't a house arrest. He was in chains. We read about it a bit in 2 Timothy:

> Remember Jesus Christ, risen from the dead, the offspring of David, as preached in my gospel, for which I am suffering, bound with chains as a criminal. But the word of God is not bound! Therefore I endure everything for the sake of the elect that they also may obtain the salvation that is in Christ Jesus with eternal glory. The saying is trustworthy, for:
>
> > If we have died with him, we will also live with him;
> > if we endure, we will also reign with him;
> > if we deny him, he also will deny us;
> > if we are faithless, he remains faithful (2 Tim. 2:8-13).

And then, at the end of 2 Timothy, in chapter 4, we hear about Demas one last time.

> Do your best to come to me soon. For *Demas*, in love with this present world, has deserted me and gone to Thessalonica (2 Tim. 4:9-10, emphasis added).

Demas, a part of the inner circle of Paul when Paul was having great success preaching the gospel and establishing local churches, deserts Paul. We don't know exactly when but given Paul's circumstances and his decision to mention him in 2 Timothy, it would appear that it came when Paul was back in Rome.

The word Paul uses for 'deserted' could also be translated 'forsaken.' The Greek word 'forsaken' (*egkataleipo*) means 'to abandon, desert, leave in straits, leave helpless, leave in the lurch, let one down.'[1] Demas has left Paul in dire straits. He is facing execution. Demas abandons Paul in his greatest time of need and leaves Rome for Thessalonica.

What a legacy for Demas. A man who walked and talked and sat and ate and ministered with Paul himself. And Mark. And Luke the doctor. What stories and testimonies must he have heard? What must he have seen: Miracles. Great conversions. He would have seen the mighty of Rome saved. And he would have seen the great persecutions and faith of believers. Demas had a front row seat to some of the greatest moments of the church age. But, in the end, he deserts Paul. And the tone suggests he deserted the Lord.

THE CONTRAST BETWEEN PAUL AND DEMAS

Consider for a minute the contrast between these two men.

Paul, at the end of his life, is giving his life for Jesus. Paul, by now, is in his early to mid 60s. He has loved Jesus more and more.

> For I am already being poured out like a drink offering, and the time for my departure is near. I have fought the good fight, I have finished the race, I have kept the faith. Now there is in store for me the crown of righteousness, which the Lord, the righteous Judge, will award to me on that day—and not only to me, but also to all who have longed for his appearing (2 Tim. 4: 6-8 NIV).

Doesn't this sound like Caleb?

> And now, behold, I am this day eighty-five years old. I am still as strong today as I was in the day that Moses sent me; my strength now is as my strength was then, for war and

---

1.   *Weust's Word Study From The New Testament*, Vol 2, Grand Rapids: William B Eerdmans, 1966.

for going and coming. So now give me this hill country of which the LORD spoke on that day, for you heard on that day how the Anakim were there, with great fortified cities. It may be that the LORD will be with me, and I shall drive them out just as the LORD said (Josh. 14:10-12).

Paul, in 2 Timothy, is writing to the effect, 'Here, at the end of a long life, I am as full of passion to take hold of my new life in God, to take hold of what God has promised and given, as I was when I began.'

Demas, however, given the chance to live that same life of passionate self-sacrifice, of pouring himself out for Jesus because of his love for Jesus, fails. And runs. And runs to the world, not Jesus. We don't know how old he was, but, given his company, he didn't appear to be young and he didn't appear to be a neophyte disciple. His name suggests he was a Gentile from Philippi. And there are names in Philippi at the time that suggest he might have come from a wealthy family. This is conjecture but even from the text, he is a man who has been discipled personally by Paul, lived with Paul, and traveled with Paul. And he deserts Paul at the end.

WHERE DID DEMAS GO WRONG?

Paul gives this reason: Demas was 'in love with this present world.'

Why did he leave? He loved the world. For all the time spent in fruitful ministry with Paul, he deserts Paul because of his love for the world.

Why Demas went to Thessalonica and what he did there is not revealed in the Scriptures. But we do know that Thessalonica was a large, prosperous Roman city. It would have been filled with great wonders and comforts and opportunities for fame and fortune. And if he came from there, perhaps he was returning to his family, not solely out of love for his family but, sadly, out of love for the world and all it had to offer there.

A church father, John Chrysostom, the preacher who lived about A.D. 400, suggests that 'having loved his own ease and security from danger, he has chosen rather to live luxuriously at home, than to suffer hardships' apparently with Paul.[2]

Polycarp, the bishop of Smyrna in the first half of the second century A.D., wrote an epistle to the church at Philippi. In the ninth chapter of his epistle, he listed some of the martyrs of the early church: Ignatius, Zosimus, Rufus, Paul and other apostles, and said that all these had not 'run in vain' because they did not 'love this present world.'[3] Polycarp hints that he is referring to Demas when he lists the martyrs and said they did not love this present world. The implication was that Demas did not want to be a martyr, so he abandoned Paul in Rome just before he was executed. If this is the case, the allurement that enticed Demas was the love of this life over the promise of eternal life. He valued his earthly life more than receiving the crown of life (James 1:12; Rev. 2:10).

WHAT IS LOVE FOR THIS PRESENT WORLD?

The idea behind the love of this present world can be inferred in I John 2:15-17. There we read:

> Do not love the world or the things of the world. If anyone loves the world, the love of the Father is not in him. For all that is in the world—the lust of the flesh, the lust of the eyes, and the pride of life—is not of the Father but is of the world. And the world is passing away, and the lust of it, but he who does the will of God abides forever.

Love for the world can be summed up in three ways:

---

2. Thomas Oden, *The Word of Life Systematic Theology*, Vol 21, p. 176.

3. *Polycarp to the Philippians* 9:1, 2; LCL I: 295.

- Lust of the flesh—The gratification of the flesh (what makes me feel good physically to excess).
- Lust of the eyes—Covetousness and cravings. Being unsatisfied with what I have. Seeing and wanting what I don't have to make me happy.
- Pride of life—This is the arrogance that people have when they boast about themselves, their accomplishments, or their possessions.

To clarify, enjoyment of the world in and of itself is not evil. We can eat and drink to the glory of God. We can enjoy material blessings to the glory of God. When we do that, we enjoy this world in such a way that God is always in view, both as the giver of the blessing and the ultimate object of our enjoyments. But it is the sinful heart that turns the world into such cravings and idols that they become the love of one's life. It is one thing to enjoy what God has given us in the world but quite another when those enjoyments and pleasures become a love that displaces God's rightful place as the source for all our enjoyment and as the true object of our love. Wasn't this at the core of the Fall? Satan, in his lies to Eve, causes Eve to see the fruit of the tree as pleasing, not pleasing as something given by God but pleasing in and of itself, so much so that Adam and Eve were willing to disobey the one commandment from God and thus forfeit their place in the garden. It was this same love of the world that results in Demas deserting the apostle Paul. And we face that same temptation to love the world today.

I am tempted to think that had I been with the great apostle, I would have followed him to the bitter end. But maybe not. Personally, as I reflect on my past, it is tempting to think of the many blessings that have come my way and to think that all is well.

- Promotions at work
- Big awards for the work done

- Children
- Grandchildren
- Good church
- Married for 40 years
- Health
- An affluent lifestyle

However, as I am honest with myself, I think I am at risk to be like Demas rather than to stay with Paul and face martyrdom. And I know why: because the love of the world is something that creeps into the heart. It doesn't explode onto my heart all at once.

The love of the world comes in a series of minute compromises, of small decisions, of minor abuses of our freedom in Christ, all of which lead me away from Jesus and into the present world. Eve didn't rebel outright against the Lord. She saw. She craved. She minimized the command. She changed the command. And she tasted.

The quote in the last chapter by Watchman Nee bears repeating:

> Ironically, this is how temptation comes in. Violate your conscience a little bit today and a little bit more tomorrow; read the Bible a little less today and just a little bit less the next; pray a few minutes less today and a few minutes less tomorrow; witness a little less today and but a trifle less the next day. This is how you slide backward. Satan will not have you stop gathering, reading the Bible, praying or witnessing all at once. No, he will instead cause you to draw back little by little. He is most patient in pulling you back only gradually.[4]

Here are some examples in my life that suggest that the love of the world is seeping into my life more and more:

---

4. Watchman Nee, *Ibid.*

Lack of financial sacrificial giving

My wife and I are affluent. We tithe or come close to it. We are even generous towards individuals and charitable organizations. But I think the Lord expects more of those who are affluent. I can afford to be generous. But that isn't sacrificial. Sacrificial means it makes an impact on the life we live, being unable to do certain things that we could otherwise do. In other words, I seem to be holding on to the wealth I have because I love having wealth.

Lack of servanthood

We are called to be servants in this life, a concept that is increasingly foreign in the United States. More than that, it is certainly not esteemed but that's what we are called to. Just as Jesus laid aside His glory, humbled Himself and became a servant, even unto death—we are called to imitate Him. But here's the challenge: I can accommodate serving within my comfortable lifestyle. Just as I can afford to be generous without it being sacrificial, I can serve without being a servant. It's one thing to do an occasional good deed. It's altogether something different to have the mindset and lifestyle of a servant.

Time spent on myself

While I serve in my own comfortable way, I am aware that the vast bulk of my time is really spent on myself. Work, at home. It's about me. And, honestly, part of me loves my life the way it is.

A stagnant relationship with Jesus

I am often comfortable with the relationship that I have with Jesus; or, to put it more bluntly, stagnant. I might go through the motions of going to church or going to a home group meeting, without having a genuinely vital relationship with Him. I might be mildly aware that there is more but I am very comfortable with where I am. I know

Him. I love Him. But I am not pressing on to know Him more. That is fertile ground for loving the world.

An indifference to the suffering of others in the world

Be it persecution of brothers and sisters in the Middle East, to abortion, to modern-day slavery, I give all that a nod but I do little or nothing about it. And I ignore the Scriptures that charge me to not turn away from the persecution of believers and injustice to the poor and the weak. And I do so in combination with the enjoyment of life with my abundance.

There are other examples but, taken together, the picture I see of myself is not like Paul, being poured out for Christ. It is too much like a man who is living comfortably in this present world. I am not denying Christ. But I am accommodating Christ within my own lifestyle. And, for me, that is a dangerous thing. It's a no man's land between the love for Jesus and the love of the world. And it is untenable.

WHAT IS THE SOLUTION?

It is tempting to give the familiar litany of solutions that we hear as Christians to a heart growing cold.

- Pray more
- Read more
- Repent
- Do not neglect the gathering of believers.

These are important elements of countering the love for the world.

But I think there also is something more fundamental. The right way to stop loving one thing is to love something else in its place and all the more. If that is correct, then I need to replace my love for the world with love for God. It takes a change of affections, from my comfort and pleasures and love of safety, to a full-on love for God. But how? How do we do that?

Here is a dynamic to consider: abiding and receiving. For all that we 'do,' the essence of a compelling relationship with Jesus is time with Him. And that involves a positioning of ourselves with Him, as well as receiving from Him.

Abiding
Consider Psalm 91.

> He who dwells in the shelter of the Most High
> will abide in the shadow of the Almighty.
> I will say to the LORD, 'My refuge and my fortress,
> my God, in whom I trust.'

Here we see the call to dwell in the shadow of the Most High. If you can picture that somehow, it becomes immediately clear that to remain under the shadow of something, you must draw close to it or him. And you must stay there. There is this notion of abiding. We draw near to God and stay close to Him. Some people have a notion of a God who is distant. That is never the case. Whether we 'feel' close to Him or not, the truth is that He is close.

We say that the clouds have chased away the sunlight but the truth is that the sun is always shining. All to say, God is near and delights when we draw near and abide with Him. That was always the plan. That is abiding: maintaining a close standing with the Lord. It can come through your devotions, but I think it also comes through the awareness of Him all day long. Notice what the Psalmist says? He abides with the Lord Who is a refuge and a fortress. Those aren't times of meditation. When you need a refuge or a fortress, stuff is happening. Whether trials at work or challenges within your family. Health issues. Money issues. Abide with the Lord.

I don't think Paul, in his last days, waited until his devotions to meet with the Lord. And we don't have to either.

Receiving

And then there's receiving. Here is the great wonder of God's love. He is already loving us. He desires for us to receive that love in greater measure. And there is no end to His love. It isn't something to be rationed. The Apostle John writes:

> See what kind of love the Father has given to us, that we should be called children of God; and so we are (1 John 3:1).

Do you want to flee from the love of the world that is growing like a cancer in your heart? Let God's love abound in your heart. It doesn't magically drive it out. But it is the greater love. The undeniable love. And, over time, it will drive love of the world to the fringes.

In a good family, children come to love their parents more and more as they grow older. And that is how it should be between us and the Lord. Early in our salvation there is a great enthusiasm for the Lord. But only as we come to see how great and faithful He is, does our love deepen and grow richer. Consider:

> You may love worldly things—but they cannot love you in return. You love gold and silver—but your gold cannot love you in return. You give away your love to the creature—and receive no love back. But if you love God, He will love you in return. 'If any man loves me, my Father will love him, and we will come unto him, and make our abode with him' (John 14:23). God will not be behind in love to us. For our *drop* of love to Him—we shall receive an *ocean!*[5] (Emphasis added.)

---

5. Thomas Watson, *All Things for Good* (Banner of Truth Trust, 1986) p. 93.

CONCLUSION

Why choose Demas in this chapter? He is such a minor character, barely referenced at all in the Bible. What does he have to do with our finishing well? Although we like to try and identify with heroes of the faith, the reality is that almost no one in our generation will be a person of great note. In the history of the church, there are few Augustines and Calvins and Luthers, Owens and Spurgeons. The vast majority of Christians will live in historical and personal obscurity. If we lived in the New Testament times of the Bible, our names wouldn't even make it into Scripture or, if they did, it would be a bare mention like the few that are mentioned in Paul's letters in greetings. Like ... Demas.

Finishing well isn't about finishing in some heroic way. It's about finishing the race full of love and faith and hope. It's persevering to the end. Finishing well means, at the end of our lives, we love God more and more as we are carried along by God's great love for us. We spend time with Him more and more. We train ourselves to see all things as coming through Him. We get to know him more. We always treasure how we came to be in fellowship through the cross.

Somehow, Demas lost sight of his loving connection with the Lord, if he ever had it. We don't really know how. In reality, we will be neither Demas nor Paul in our pilgrimage here on earth. We will be ourselves. But how our journey ends depends on all the choices we make and who we make our true love. It's that simple. What will we choose to love and give ourselves to? The world, like Demas? Or Jesus, like Paul?

7

Paul

and Resisting Factions
in the Church and the World

We allow theological differences instead of the love of God to determine the quality, openness and depth of our relationship. We part company convinced that the real problem is theological, when, in fact, we have managed, by our very detachment to prevent the love of God from bringing harmony and mutual acceptance. We then declare that our theological differences are the cause of the schism between us.[1] (David Prior)

INTRODUCTION

This chapter was originally given as a sermon to the Winers at the beach before President Trump was elected. The direction of the country since then only reinforces the challenges we face as Christians living in these times, for they say something about what is happening to us as a country and to us as individuals. We are more polarized. More angry. More divided.

From the 'Tea Party' to 'Occupy DC' to 'Black Lives Matter' to 'Alt right white supremacy groups,' we see more and more factions emerging. This fracturing isn't

---

1. David Prior, *The Message of 1 Corinthians*, Part of The *Bible Speaks Today* Commentary (Intervarsity Press, 1985), p. 31.

restricted to the extremes, however. Whether in politics or society as a whole, more and more people are coalescing around separate banners of politics, religion, environment, ethnicity, class or age. And personally, as we get older, our views and opinions and loyalties tend to coalesce and harden. Our strong feelings are fed by experience, learning, and passion. It becomes easier for us to decide that some are right and some are wrong and slip into a clique or faction.

Quite frankly, Christians have been as susceptible to factionalism and division as anyone else. Even in the little church I belonged to, there was a certain degree of factionalism. The group that went to the beach for these messages was comprised of the older members of the church. We were part of the charismatic movement more than others who came after us. We were the members who supposedly had the most wisdom (which was certainly debatable). We were part of the group that had either founded the church or were early members who helped firm its foundations. All of that made us a distinct group, a clique. While we worked hard to avoid it, there certainly were cliques in our church.

However, the phenomenon of factions in our church was minor compared to other churches or denominations. We see churches breaking apart on the issues of the role of women, sexual orientation, charismatic practices, and worship practices. The fact that there are so many denominations and flavors within denominations alone makes the point that we are prone to form cliques. It is incipient in any group that grows to any size.

The question to ask is, what is the effect of all that? Certainly, we need to consider the problem of division and factionalism. And as we get older, it is important to consider what our will legacy will be. But most importantly, what will the Lord say of us? Is there a better way?

FACTIONS IN THE CHURCH

The idea of factions has been part of the church as long as the church has existed. It became such a problem in one New Testament church that Paul had to address it head on because it was threatening to undermine both the church and the gospel that was being preached. We read how he addresses it in 1 Corinthians 1. The church there was large, with a contingent of wealthy Corinthians. Many great teachers had been there, including Paul and Apollos. They experienced significant charismatic expressions, including prophecies and speaking in tongues. Despite the clear work of the Holy Spirit there, Paul had to write and deliver a strong message of correction. And it began with the factions that were there.

> Paul, called by the will of God to be an apostle of Christ Jesus, and our brother Sosthenes,
>
> To the church of God that is in Corinth, to those sanctified in Christ Jesus, called to be saints together with all those who in every place call upon the name of our Lord Jesus Christ, both their Lord and ours: Grace to you and peace from God our Father and the Lord Jesus Christ.
>
> I give thanks to my God always for you because of the grace of God that was given you in Christ Jesus, that in every way you were enriched in him in all speech and all knowledge—even as the testimony about Christ was confirmed among you—so that you are not lacking in any spiritual gift, as you wait for the revealing of our Lord Jesus Christ, who will sustain you to the end, guiltless in the day of our Lord Jesus Christ. God is faithful, by whom you were called into the fellowship of his Son, Jesus Christ our Lord.
>
> *I appeal to you, brothers, by the name of our Lord Jesus Christ, that all of you agree, and that there be no divisions among you, but that you be united in the same mind and the same judgment.* For it has been reported to me by Chloe's people that there is quarreling among you, my brothers.

What I mean is that each one of you says, 'I follow Paul,' or 'I follow Apollos,' or 'I follow Cephas,' or 'I follow Christ.' Is Christ divided? Was Paul crucified for you? Or were you baptized in the name of Paul? I thank God that I baptized none of you except Crispus and Gaius, so that no one may say that you were baptized in my name. (I did baptize also the household of Stephanas. Beyond that, I do not know whether I baptized anyone else.) For Christ did not send me to baptize but to preach the gospel, and not with words of eloquent wisdom, lest the cross of Christ be emptied of its power (1 Cor. 1:1-17, emphasis added).

THE TENDENCY TOWARDS FACTIONS

Paul identifies four factions at the church of Corinth. Some or all may sound familiar in your own church. David Prior gives us an excellent summary of them.

The Paul Faction

Many at this church were strongly attached to Paul. He had brought them to faith and they were forever in his debt. The total transformation God had effected in their lives, from the darkness of utter paganism to the marvelous light of the gospel, made them doubly grateful for Paul's labor on their behalf. So whatever Paul said or was imagined to have said, these folks accepted verbatim. They probably regarded everyone else as second rate anyway, his memory lived on. They had taken their eyes off the Lord in the passage of time and are consequently harking back to the good ol' days.[2]

The Apollos Faction

When Apollos came to Corinth with his intellectual ability, his fine speaking, his expository skill in the Old Testament Scriptures, his accurate teaching about Jesus, his fervent enthusiasm, his powerful confrontation of the

---

2. Prior, *Ibid*, pp. 30-31.

Jews in public and his bold preaching—it is no wonder he attracted a following.[3]

Some feel that Apollos, with such a background, might have been unwittingly responsible for the creation for *introducing something of an intellectual elite in Corinth.*[4] (Emphasis added.)

The Christ Faction

Whenever the Spirit of God is at work, there always emerges a group of folks who always sit very lightly indeed to any human leadership... hero worship was anathema. *Who needs leaders anyway? Christ is our leader, He is the head of the body. We depend on him alone and we go straight to him...* This party would have given considerable emphasis to Gnostic tendencies at Corinth. Whereas the Apollos group could have been responsible for introducing an intellectual elite into the Corinthian church, *this group would have spawned a super spiritual elite.*[5] (Emphasis added.)

The Peter Faction

[They] represented Jewish Christianity in some form. There is ample evidence of legalistic tendencies in the church at Corinth, particularly in the debate about the rights and wrongs in the eating of food sacrificed to idols...the temptation to return to legalism must have been very strong, especially in the notorious profligacy of Corinthian society.'[6]

So here we see the ingredients for factions:

- A strong identification with a particular leader and his teachings, way of life.

---

3. Prior, *Ibid*, p. 32.
4. Prior, *Ibid*, p. 32.
5. Prior, *Ibid*, p. 34.
6. Prior, *Ibid*, p. 33.

- A deep emphasis on some deeply held tenets of Scripture over the deeply held tenets of another group.
- A sense of having a superior understanding of how life should be in the local church.
- Setting oneself apart from others in the practice of faith.

What is particularly difficult when it comes to factions is that there is a nub of truth in each faction. Of course Paul should be respected. Of course Peter should be respected. Of course we esteem Christ. Of course we respect other teachers. But when that kernel of truth begins to exclude the value of other truths and exalt its own viewpoint, factions spring up. Whether out of jealousy or pride or self-righteousness or defensiveness or a sense of power or lack of power, factions take root in that truth but become untruthful and divisive in full bloom.

THE HARM OF FACTIONS

You would think that Paul might at least have something good to say about the Paul faction. After all, he was the one calling the Corinthians out; wouldn't his followers be in the right? Or what could be wrong with the Christ faction? If anyone was doing it right, certainly it would have to be that group, yes? In fact, Paul has nothing good to say about these factions. Quite the opposite.

> I appeal to you, brothers, by the name of our Lord Jesus Christ, that all of you agree, and that there be no divisions among you, but that you be united in the same mind and the same judgment (1 Cor. 1:10, emphasis added).

He sees all factions as the source of division, quarrels. And clearly they are the basis for the many unbiblical practices that he needs to correct. It is not just that they quarrel, but that they invalidate the power of the gospel; they demean Jesus \ Himself.

They are fed by and produce the fruit of spiritual pride. We think we know better than others. We mistake our knowledge for spiritual wisdom. And divisions form.

They diminish the full message of the gospel. While emphasizing some aspect of gospel life, they drain the truth and power of the gospel by elevating the part over the whole. And the gospel in part is not the gospel.

Factions divide. They inhibit the power of the message of the cross in community by mimicking the divisions that occur in sinful man, only they do it within the church.

> We allow theological differences instead of the love of God to determine the quality, openness and depth of our relationship...We part company convinced that the real problem is theological, when, in fact, we have managed, by our very detachment to prevent the love of God from bringing harmony and mutual acceptance. We then declare that our theological differences are the cause of the schism between us.[7]

AM I IN A FACTION?

Frankly, the question isn't, 'Am I in a faction', but 'What faction am I in?' Perhaps you already can think of a faction or factions you belong to. If you can't, try this: think about groups of people in the church that you don't agree with, that you feel separated from, that you wish would become more like you. That is the dynamic of factionalism.

Paul identifies four specific groups in Corinth but we shouldn't think this is a comprehensive list. Let me suggest one additional group, for example: The Church Pundit Faction. It works like those Sunday morning talk shows where a group of commentators tear into the groups with which they disagree with a degree of sophistication

---

7. Prior, *Ibid*, p. 31.

that actually serves as a veneer for self-importance. It is intellectual mockery for sport and influence. In the church, the Church Pundits are characterized as follows:

- Able to easily discern and criticize the shortcomings of the church and its leaders
- Able to state authoritatively how things could be better
- Don't own any faults of their own, at least none that are as serious as the others
- Often done in a cynical or judgmental tone that is mixed with sympathy and concern

Whereas Paul's groups were identified by following someone else—Paul, Apollos, Jesus, Peter—the Church Pundit follows himself or herself. 'I follow the perfect leader who is in my own head.'

THE BETTER WAY

The need to combat factionalism is essential. It's not something to be tolerated or excused. Paul himself has nothing good to say about any of the factions in Corinth. He makes an even stronger appeal in Ephesians 4:1-6:

> I therefore, a prisoner for the Lord, urge you to walk in a manner worthy of the calling to which you have been called, with all humility and gentleness, with patience, bearing with one another in love, *eager to maintain the unity of the Spirit in the bond of peace.* There is one body and one Spirit—just as you were called to the one hope that belongs to your call—one Lord, one faith, one baptism, one God and Father of all, who is over all and through all and in all. (Emphasis added.)

Paul is not saying that we become some mindless group of Stepford Christians, agreeing perfectly on all things, all living the exact same way. But he is saying that despite whatever differences we may have, we make every effort to maintain the unity of the Spirit in the bond of peace. Mature Christians should be marked by their willingness to stay together in love and fellowship despite their differences. It should be only in the most extreme of cases—doctrinal error on the essentials of faith, toleration of serious sin, unhealthy elevation of leaders over the authority of Scripture—that we should separate from each other.

Paul's plea for unity in the church recognizes that while differences will exist among believers, divisions are not acceptable in the kingdom of heaven. Divisiveness and division are antithetical to the entire message of reconciliation embedded in the gospel. It is folly to think that there will be divisions in heaven. And should we not be practicing unity here on earth in anticipation of the life to come?

Furthermore, division among Christians undermines the witness of the gospel. It indicates serious heart issues between believers. How can we preach the love of Christ and the command to love another deeply from the heart when we stand apart on our particular cause, tradition, or practice? Non-Christians see such division and strife and rightly ask themselves, 'Why would I want to be like them?'

Repent of the sins leading to division
The way out of factionalism begins with repentance. Factionalism usually has a kernel of truth embedded in it but sin is at the core of factionalism. And in order to change, one must repent. Here are two of the more common sins embedded in factionalism.

Spiritual pride—Cynicism, superiority. A sense of having a better wisdom and thinking more highly of yourself for it.

Lack of love—My need to be right trumps God's command to love one another as Christ loves us, even when there is conflict.

Prize and Pursue Kingdom Unity
But genuine repentance is not just a turning away from sin. It is also a turning to right living. And when it comes to division, the law of love must be the only right way to love one another. Practice the law of love in times of conflict and disagreement. That law of love is perfectly outlined in 1 Corinthians 13:4-8:

> Love is patient and kind; love does not envy or boast; it is not arrogant or rude. It does not insist on its own way; it is not irritable or resentful; it does not rejoice at wrongdoing, but rejoices with the truth. Love bears all things, believes all things, hopes all things, endures all things. Love never ends.

Adopt a humble attitude about yourself
Don't be deceived. God hates ungodly pride. In fact, He doesn't just hate it; He despises it. Consider just this sampling:

> Everyone who is arrogant in heart is an abomination to the LORD; be assured, he will not go unpunished (Prov. 16:5).

> The fear of the LORD is hatred of evil. Pride and arrogance and the way of evil and perverted speech I hate (Prov. 8:13).

> Therefore it says, 'God opposes the proud but gives grace to the humble' (James 4:6).

Before engaging in divisiveness based on your proud assessment of others' wrongs and your rightness, search your heart deep and long. If pride is mixed up in your righteousness, then be advised, God opposes you.

To be humbled by being accepted by God necessarily demands that we reconsider our position towards others. Does it make any sense that we might bow humbly before God while exalting ourselves above others? Shall we be like the man in the temple who bows before God humbly and thanks Him that he is not like the beggar beside him? Is that the example Jesus set for us when He was here on earth? When we humble ourselves before God, we cannot exalt ourselves, including our precious opinions, our sacred cows, above others.

Biblical humility causes us to be suspicious of our own hearts when we move into the realm of division and divisiveness. If you are engaged in a debate or disagreement with others that is dividing your church, you must first start by examining your own heart for signs of pride in how you engage with those you disagree with.

Humility also quickly acknowledges that we don't know as much as we would like to think that we do. Our own opinions may not be as well thought out biblically as we think. And we may not know everything about others. The more we learn about a matter, the more we see the need for wisdom. That is the way of humility.

Humility also endeavors to honor and think well of others. It replaces suspicion with graciousness and respect. If Jesus loved your opponent enough to die for him or her, does it make any sense that you would think poorly of him or her? This is God's beloved son or daughter. Let's treat that person with the respect they are due in Christ.

Adopt a loving, patient attitude towards others

Genuine love for others means that we will be lovingly patient towards them when there is disagreement. Just as the Lord is patient with us when we go astray, so we must be patient with others when there is a temptation to separate.

Patience is far more nuanced than we think. It isn't simple endurance until someone comes around. The loving patience of 1 Corinthians 13 is charitable and kind.

One of the greatest events in U.S. history was the Civil War, a terrible tragedy costing hundreds of thousands of lives. The country was divided in a war for its very existence. Near the end of the war, in his Second Inaugural Address in 1865, Abraham Lincoln, looking forward to the need for the country to come back together when the war was over, said this:

> *With malice toward none, with charity for all, with firmness in the right as God gives us to see the right,* let us strive on to finish the work we are in, to bind up the nation's wounds, to care for him who shall have borne the battle and for his widow and his orphan, to do all which may achieve and cherish a just and lasting peace among ourselves and with all nations.[8] (Emphasis added.)

Stop and consider. Men had engaged in warfare against each other. Killed and wounded. Burned and inflicted lifelong terrors. Yet Lincoln recognized that the patience to heal the nation would require the lack of malice, charity for the other and a firmness to bear with one another. Sadly, the country failed to take up this challenge. The church must and can do better.

Loving patience can be summarized in the phrase, 'In essentials, unity; in non-essentials, liberty; in all things, charity.' Such an approach to our brothers and sisters requires patience with a loving disposition. There is no room for wounded pride or spiritual superiority. We must be united on the essentials of our faith. But let us also give liberty to others on non-essentials and treat all charitably through it all. That is the essence of loving patience.

Adopt a grateful attitude towards others

The letter to the Corinthians is a clear rebuke, but look how Paul begins the letter in 1 Corinthians 1 right before he begins his appeal against divisions:

---

8. Abraham Lincoln, Second Inaugural Address, March 4, 1865, https://en.wikipedia.org/wiki/Abraham_Lincoln%27s_second_inaugural_address.

> I give thanks to my God always for you because of the grace of God that was given you in Christ Jesus, that in every way you were enriched in him in all speech and all knowledge—even as the testimony about Christ was confirmed among you—so that you are not lacking in any gift, as you wait for the revealing of our Lord Jesus Christ, who will sustain you to the end, guiltless in the day of our Lord Jesus Christ. God is faithful, by whom you were called into the fellowship of his Son, Jesus Christ our Lord (1 Cor. 1:4-9).

Paul's view of the Corinthians was founded in gratitude towards them because of the grace of God in them. That's how he really viewed them. He didn't start out by calling them difficult or sinners or divisive. He viewed them as brothers and sisters in Christ, recipients of the same grace he had received himself. And it allowed him to speak to them in an entirely different manner. His letter wasn't filled with self-righteous denunciations of others or self-righteous anger towards others. It was written out of loving concern for fellow believers who had fallen into sinful and misguided practices. And that's how we need to deal with difficult people and people with whom we disagree.

Think of someone you know, a Christian brother or sister, who is difficult to be with. Maybe they are even living in some sinful kind of way. Maybe they are immature. Maybe they have wrong doctrinal beliefs. You find it difficult to be around them. Got a person in mind? Are you thankful for [fill in the blank with their name]? Are you grateful for them because, for no other reason, 'of the grace of God that was given [him or her] in Christ Jesus, that in every way [he or she] was enriched in him ...' If you aren't thankful, you've failed Paul's call to bear with each other in love and unity.

HOW DOES UNITY LOOK IN THE LOCAL CHURCH AND AMONG BELIEVERS?

In deciding to love Jesus and live for Him, it is essential to maintain the unity of the body of the local church. Here are a few ways that is worked out.

Irenic in our disagreements

It is obvious that there will be disagreements between us. But how we conduct ourselves during those disagreements often is more important to the Lord than the actual disagreement.

Irenic means aiming or aimed at peace. Christians will disagree. But that disagreement must be moderated by our love for Christ and each other.

Here is a wonderful list of ways in which the Puritan, Ralph Venning, describes the law of love at work in the church.[9] It serves as a most useful guide to conduct ourselves in disagreements and avoid division:

- Labor for a right understanding of each other's mind.
- When you begin to talk to each other, deal faithfully as in the presence of God.
- Be as willing to listen as to speak. A man should listen twice as much as he speaks.
- Weigh not who speaks but weigh what is spoken.
- When truth is spoken by someone else, yield to it.
- Bear with one another in love.
- Until you are agreed, have charitable thoughts, not hard and harsh judgments.
- Do not withdraw your love from someone when God does not withdraw His love from that man.
- Do not doubt a man's intentions until, by his actions, he reveals his meaning.

9. *The Puritans on Loving One Another*, (Soli Deo Gloria Publishers, 1997), pp 7-31.

- Do nothing to provoke or exasperate one another. Provoke others to love as much as you can and exasperate others as little as you can.
- Grant to others what you would have them grant to you.
- Do all that you can so you can agree.

Having a loving attitude towards everyone instead of thinking less of them

We must see these foolish factions the way Paul sees them. Bryan Chappell writes:

> God pities rather than scorns believers for the wrongs in our lives. Thus, his treatment of our failures is motivated by mercy rather than by cruelty or contempt.[10]

If that is the case, then should we do no less? Shall we scorn others in the church because they don't measure up to our standards? Or shall we *extend the abundant mercy that God extends to us to them, knowing that whatever mercy that we extend is immeasurably smaller than what we receive from Him*?

Do we scorn others because they don't value what we value? Are we bitter that others have prevailed? Or angry because another faction has harmed us? Do we scorn others because they reject our wisdom? Or do we show them love and patience because God does not reject us when we think more highly of ourselves than we should?

CONCLUSION

There is no way to finish well before God when we contribute to the disrepute brought to our Savior through factions and division.

---

10. Bryan Chappell, *Holiness by Grace: Delighting In The Joy That Is Our Strength* (Crossway Press, 2001), p. 195.

Everyone has a good opinion of his or her own opinion. I know I love my opinions far more than I should. But if I allow my opinions to trump loving my brother and sister, then I cannot glorify God. And that is the ultimate goal. John gets to this in John 13:31-35:

> When he had gone out, Jesus said, 'Now is the Son of Man glorified, and God is glorified in him. If God is glorified in him, God will also glorify him in himself, and glorify him at once. Little children, yet a little while I am with you. You will seek me, and just as I said to the Jews, so now I also say to you, "Where I am going you cannot come." A new commandment I give to you, that you love one another: just as I have loved you, you also are to love one another. By this all people will know that you are my disciples, if you have love for one another.'

We must give up the supremacy of our opinions in light of the new command from the Lord to love each other as Jesus loved us. And it is this way that the world will witness our difference from the rest of this fractured world.

As we move into the final season of life, how does your life in the church look? Are you one who promotes genuine love and peace and unity or are you part of the crowd that is anxious to promote its particular brand of Christian living? As we grow older, younger generations look to us as examples of a mature Christian life and for sound doctrine lived well. What is the example that you are teaching when it comes to disagreements and differences and factions? Are you so convinced of the rightness of your opinions and beliefs that the church is divided?

And it isn't limited to church matters and personalities. Are you so consumed with your political views that you can no longer live out the command to love your enemies? What do others see when politics come up or hot button issues like abortion or gay rights? Or are you committed to the law of love that glorifies the Lord and softens hard hearts that allows those who disagree with you to hear the gospel?

Everyone is tempted to fall on their sword for some cause, some belief, or some group. But as Christians, we aren't called to fall on our sword; we are called to follow the One who bore our cross. First and foremost, we aren't Democrats or Republicans. We aren't liberals or conservatives. Paul would never have allowed himself to be pigeonholed that way. And Jesus certainly could never be labeled by the religious parties of His times. As we grow older, we need to have the wisdom to understand who we really are. Otherwise, we are no different from anyone else. And that is not how we should end.

8
Joshua
and How Memorials Help us Finish Well

INTRODUCTION

In this chapter, we will look back at a biblical practice that I think has merit for finishing well. It isn't a command and we don't see it in the New Testament, so it should be taken as good advice that *could* help us finish our lives well.

In Chapter 1, I mentioned that I had run several Marine Corps Marathons. At the end of the race, a Marine greets you, removes the timing chip from your shoe, gives you a foil blanket, and hangs a medallion around your neck. I've run the race three times. Those medallions remind me of those races.

There are other items that remind me of successes or meaningful times and people in my life. For example, I was awarded the IRS Commissioner's award. It's the highest award you can receive in the IRS. It was given to me because of my service as the Director of the Executive Secretariat. I also have a display showing the medals my father was awarded while in the Air Force. They include the Distinguished Flying Cross, one of the top medals awarded to members of the Air Force. And there are certain pictures in our house that remind us of special family times and certain ways that we have enjoyed each other over the years.

Let me suggest that tangible memorials like this can help us finish well. We will come back to them later but they serve to introduce Joshua to us.

JOSHUA AND THE MEMORIALS TO GOD

Joshua was a contemporary of Caleb, whom we considered as we introduced this book. Like Caleb, he was one of the spies Moses sent into the Promised Land. Like Caleb, he brought back a positive report. Like Caleb, God spared him from the rest of his generation of Israelites and allowed him to enter the Promised Land after the rest, except Caleb, had died in the wilderness.

Joshua was the anointed leader of Israel when Moses died. He was the one who led Israel into the Promised Land and who led the battles to secure the land. And that is what we want to look at in this chapter.

Throughout the book of Joshua, from the time they crossed the Jordan into the Promised Land, throughout their campaigns to defeat the Lord's enemies to take the land, at key moments in Israel's history Joshua erects monuments or memorials or altars to mark the occasions. Sometimes it is a victory. Sometimes it is a key event.

In this chapter, we will look briefly at four of these instances to see how those monuments encourage us to create our own monuments and how that helps us finish well.

Israel Crosses The Jordan—God Is Mighty And Able To Do All That He Has Promised
The first instance is when Israel crosses the Jordan River. Here, at long last, after forty years of being in the desert, with an entire generation of Israelites gone, forbidden by

God from entering because of their unbelief, finally, Israel is going to enter the land.

What a moment it must have been. This land, long promised—they were finally entering in.

Consider the excitement. They had heard the stories of the Red Sea opening but they hadn't experienced it themselves. Now, now they were about to see the power of God in a similar miracle.

At the same time, it was also a moment of trepidation. They knew they would have to take the land by force. Although hardened by their desert experience, they would have to fight to take the land. It was not going to be a light and easy experience. Men were going to fight and die. Families would experience loss. What would they find? What was going to happen next?

Between them and the land was a river that had to be crossed. The Jordan River. There would be many rivers to cross, but this one was the most important one. It separated them from the land. Across the river they had to go. Many of you know the story. Here's the description in Joshua 3:

> So when the people set out from their tents to pass over the Jordan with the priests bearing the ark of the covenant before the people, and as soon as those bearing the ark had come as far as the Jordan, and the feet of the priests bearing the ark were dipped in the brink of the water (now the Jordan overflows all its banks throughout the time of harvest), the waters coming down from above stood and rose up in a heap very far away, at Adam, the city that is beside Zarethan, and those flowing down toward the Sea of the Arabah, the Salt Sea, were completely cut off. And the people passed over opposite Jericho (Josh. 3:14-16).

The Jordan River parts miraculously. Just like the Red Sea, God parts the waters and allows them to cross over. And then we read about something peculiar in Joshua 4. Not only do they cross but they take stones out of the river bed.

And when the priests bearing the ark of the covenant of the LORD came up from the midst of the Jordan, and the soles of the priests' feet were lifted up on dry ground, the waters of the Jordan returned to their place and overflowed all its banks, as before ...

And those twelve stones, which they took out of the Jordan, Joshua set up at Gilgal. And he said to the people of Israel, 'When your children ask their fathers in times to come, "What do these stones mean?" *then you shall let your children know, "Israel passed over this Jordan on dry ground."* For the LORD your God dried up the waters of the Jordan for you until you passed over, as the LORD your God did to the Red Sea, which he dried up for us until we passed over, *so that all the peoples of the earth may know that the hand of the LORD is mighty, that you may fear the LORD your God forever'* (Josh. 4: 18-24, emphasis added).

What an event. The river parts, just as it had with Moses, and the people enter. They finally enter in but, oh, what a way to enter! The stories of old become their story. It wasn't just their parents' generation that saw the waters part; it was their generation who saw it as well.

It was such an event, God instructs them to build a monument, a memorial of stones from the Jordan River. Joshua explains that the memorial will remind all of Israel that the Lord is with them in all they do and that He is mighty and able to bring about all that He has promised.

Alexander MacClaren explains,

We often think of the Jews as monsters of ingratitude; but we should more truly learn the lesson of their history, if we regarded them as fair, average men, and asked ourselves whether our recollection of God's goodness to us is much more vivid than theirs. Unless we make distinct and frequent efforts to recall, we shall certainly forget 'all His benefits.' The cultivation of thankful remembrance is a very large part of practical religion; and it is not by accident that the Psalmist puts it in the middle, between hope and obedience, when he says 'that they might set their hope in God, and not forget the works of God, but keep His commandments' (Psalm 78:7).[1]

We've all had our own passing through moment—the most glorious moment of salvation.

Spurgeon says,

I shall never forget the memorials I set up when passing through conviction of sin; and I know that all of you remember the twelve stones you set up on the 'happy day' when you found the Savior.[2]

That quote challenges me. What are my twelve stones, symbolizing my passing from death to life? Symbolizing entering into the Promised Land? I am a very forgetful man, with a brain full of holes about the past like Swiss cheese. Do I have any monuments to God's grace of salvation, a token of God's mighty hand, that I might remind myself and tell others of the great work of God in my life?

Do you? If not, read on. Someone does.

The Altar After Ai—A Reminder Of God's Commandments

After crossing the Jordan, Israel commences the defeat of the kingdoms in the land. They defeat Jericho. And after an initial defeat, they conquer Ai. So, in short order, two great victories. Israel is on a roll. The impulse is to keep going. Instill fear into the next enemy. Instead ... Joshua builds an altar:

---

1. Alexander MacClaren, *MacClaren's Commentary – Expositions of Holy Scripture* (Delmarva Publications, 2013).

2. Charles Spurgeon, *What the Stones Say or Sermons in Stone* (Christian Herald Publishing, 1894).

> At that time Joshua built an altar to the LORD, the God of Israel, on Mount Ebal... And there, in the presence of the people of Israel, he wrote on the stones a copy of the law of Moses, which he had written. And all Israel, sojourner as well as native born, with their elders and officers and their judges, stood on opposite sides of the ark before the Levitical priests who carried the ark of the covenant of the LORD... to bless the people of Israel. And afterward he read all the words of the law, the blessing and the curse, according to all that is written in the Book of the Law (Josh. 8:30-34).

This is another noteworthy event. Here, just after a great victory, Joshua erects an altar to rededicate the Israelites to the covenant. The blessings of obedience and the curses of disobedience are read. The Israelites have heard them before but here they have particular significance.

Just think what the mood must have been among the Jews. Two great victories. Imagine the confidence and excitement. The impulse clearly must have been to keep going. Keep fighting. Keep winning. But before they go any further, they stop and remind themselves of what they are about. The temptation to think about the successes and the prospect of future successes can cause them to forget the reason they are there, who brought them there, and the conditions for that.

It is tempting for us when we are in a season of great success to revel in that success, to think that it is because of what we have done, and that future success is dependent on us, not the Lord. We can even think that the successes will keep coming.

Joshua stops the people and essentially says,
'No!'
'It isn't because you are so great.'
'It isn't because you are so mighty.'
'It's not about the cities you have conquered.'
'It's about the Lord and His covenant with His people.'

Reading the blessings and the curses was meant to remind them of Who is in charge, of how success and curses are based on their hearts towards Him, not on their talents and accomplishments in the world.

That is an important altar.

Similarly, it is good for us to stop once in a while in our own lives. To recommit ourselves to the new covenant. To remember who gives us our successes. To not be more enamored with our success and prosperity than we are of Jesus, our Lord and Savior.

What markers do we have that remind us of who He is? And who it is who is giving us the victories in our lives?

My friend Glenn lost his job many years ago. He was out of work for seven months and it was a trying time. Glenn prayed and trusted God. Those times tried him but they didn't shake his faith. Eventually, Glenn got another job. And he decided to create a type of monument to God's faithfulness. Each year, Glenn and his wife invite a few of his friends to his 'Glenn Still Has a Job Dinner.' The same group gathers each year and celebrates that Glen still has a job. But more importantly, Glen celebrates God's care and provision. That's the real point of the dinner. We are glad Glen has a job, of course. But we are even more grateful that we have a Father who takes care of us and provides for us.

That's a memorial worth building.

The Altar Of The Reubenites, Gaddites, And Half Tribe of Manasseh—The Reminder Of Peace

Once the Promised Land was largely subdued, Joshua divides the land among the Israelite tribes. A particular allotment goes to the so-called Eastern Tribes—the people of Reuben, Gad and the half tribe of Manasseh. Before Israel crossed the Jordan, they asked Moses if they could have the lands to the east of the Jordan. They had large herds of livestock and that land was suitable for them.

Moses agreed to this, provided they still crossed over the Jordan and fought for the remaining tribes, which they agreed to do.

When Joshua is dividing the land, he tells the eastern tribes that they are released to return to the land Moses had given them. They do so, but then a critical event occurs. Upon returning, they build an altar by the Jordan. A very large altar. This alarms the remaining Israelite tribes, who are immediately suspicious of the eastern tribes' intentions. They suspect that the eastern tribes have turned away from the Lord. They remember Achan's sin. They fear not only that the eastern tribes have fallen away but that God will hold all of Israel responsible for the transgression and deal with the entire nation.

The Israelites gather against the eastern tribes to make war. But before they do, they meet with the eastern tribes to understand what was done and why. We read in Joshua 22:

> And they came to the people of Reuben, the people of Gad, and the half-tribe of Manasseh, in the land of Gilead, and they said to them, 'Thus says the whole congregation of the LORD, "What is this breach of faith that you have committed against the God of Israel in turning away this day from following the LORD by building yourselves an altar this day in rebellion against the LORD?"' (Josh. 22:15-16).

The eastern tribes explain that, contrary to turning away from the Lord, the altar was meant to symbolize that the Jordan River didn't separate them as a people. It was a marker that served as a witness that they were all one people who served the Lord.

> No, but we did it from fear that in time to come your children might say to our children, 'What have you to do with the LORD, the God of Israel? For the LORD has made the Jordan a boundary between us and you, you people of Reuben and people of Gad. You have no portion in the LORD.' So your children might make our children cease

to worship the LORD. Therefore we said, 'Let us now build an altar, not for burnt offering, nor for sacrifice, *but to be a witness between us and you, and between our generations after us, that we do perform the service of the LORD in his presence with our burnt offerings and sacrifices and peace offerings, so your children will not say to our children in time to come, "You have no portion in the LORD." And we thought, 'If this should be said to us or to our descendants in time to come, we should say, "Behold, the copy of the altar of the LORD, which our fathers made, not for burnt offerings, nor for sacrifice, but to be a witness between us and you."'* ... The people of Reuben and the people of Gad called the altar Witness, 'For,' they said, 'it is a witness between us that the LORD is God' (Josh. 22:24-34, emphasis added).

The altar stands as a reminder that even though we are separate, we are all servants of the same Lord.

Those beach getaways that I mentioned at the beginning of this book, in their own way, have come to symbolize that meaning among us. Though we are separated now into different churches, we are all servants of the Lord. Gatherings like this among good Christian friends serve as a reminder that though other churches and believers might not be exactly like us, we all serve under the same marker, the cross. We've had some big debates in our time. Some big differences. But we are still together.

This kind of monument helps us not to rush to judgment. It helps us not to think poorly of other groups. It helps us to get the facts before we render judgment. It helps us to maintain the unity of the body of Christ.

At our most recent get together at the beach, I handed out something else that would serve as a memorial. It wouldn't have any meaning to anyone outside our group. But it would have all the meaning in the world to everyone in the group. It was a group portrait from years before. It was large enough to be framed. As you looked at each couple, there were reminders of wonderful times. And of hard times. Each person, each couple had a story. But we all stood together. And that was its own story. After all these years, after all we had been through, we were still together.

The Final Altar—Remember Who You Have Chosen To Serve

The final monument comes when Joshua calls the people together one last time to remind them of the story of their people, from Abraham to Moses, from the time that Abraham came to Canaan to when Moses delivered them. He calls on them to serve the Lord.

> 'Now therefore fear the LORD and serve him in sincerity and in faithfulness. Put away the gods that your fathers served beyond the River and in Egypt, and serve the LORD. And if it is evil in your eyes to serve the LORD, choose this day whom you will serve, whether the gods your fathers served in the region beyond the River, or the gods of the Amorites in whose land you dwell. But as for me and my house, we will serve the LORD.'
>
> Then the people answered, 'Far be it from us that we should forsake the LORD to serve other gods, for it is the LORD our God who brought us and our fathers up from the land of Egypt, out of the house of slavery, and who did those great signs in our sight and preserved us in all the way that we went, and among all the peoples through whom we passed. And the LORD drove out before us all the peoples, the Amorites who lived in the land. Therefore we also will serve the LORD, for he is our God.'
>
> But Joshua said to the people, 'You are not able to serve the LORD, for he is a holy God. He is a jealous God; he will not forgive your transgressions or your sins. If you forsake the LORD and serve foreign gods, then he will turn and do you harm and consume you, after having done you good.' And the people said to Joshua, 'No, but we will serve the LORD.'

Then Joshua said to the people, 'You are witnesses against yourselves that you have chosen the Lord, to serve him.' And the people said to Joshua, 'The Lord our God we will serve, and his voice we will obey.'

So Joshua made a covenant with the people that day, and put in place statutes and rules for them at Shechem. And Joshua wrote these words in the Book of the Law of God. And he took a large stone and set it up there under the terebinth that was by the sanctuary of the Lord. And Joshua said to all the people, 'Behold, this stone shall be a witness against us, for it has heard all the words of the Lord that he spoke to us. Therefore it shall be a witness against you, lest you deal falsely with your God' (Josh. 24:14-27).

It is interesting that Joshua calls on the people to renew the covenant. God had already made a covenant with them. But they are called on to renew it.

God knew their hearts. He knew they were prone to wander. Prone to turn away. He was cautioning them, 'Don't forget. Don't forget Who I Am, What I have done. And what you have committed yourselves to, to serve Me and Me only.'

In fact, they were going to wander. And soon. The age of the Judges would start with Joshua's death. So the monument of stone is a reminder of that covenant: Be true to God.

Alexander Maclaren says,

If God be 'holy' and 'jealous', serving Him must demand the forsaking of all other gods, and the surrender of heart and self to Him. That is as true to-day as ever it was. The people accept the stringent requirement, and their repeated shout of obedience has a deeper tone than their first hasty utterance had. They have learned what service means,—that it includes more than ceremonies; and they are willing to obey His voice. Blessed those for whom the plain disclosure of all that they must give up to follow

Him, only leads to the more assured and hearty response of willing surrender![3]

We do the same thing when we preach the gospel to ourselves. We are already saved and being saved by God. But it is good to 'renew' that salvation by rehearsing the gospel again and again and again.

But there is another way, one instituted by God Himself. Communion. Communion is that shared meal with Jesus and with each other. We remember the sacrifice. And we remember what was accomplished by that sacrifice. It both humbles us and thrills us.

Communion is a bulwark against forgetting the covenant, or, perhaps more realistically, not forgetting but making it to be less than it is.

WHY ARE MONUMENTS IMPORTANT?

Why write about this? We aren't commanded to set up altars or memorials or monuments. But there is a good case for them. Let me repeat Alexander McClaren:

> Unless we make distinct and frequent efforts to recall, we shall certainly forget 'all His benefits.' The cultivation of thankful remembrance is a very large part of practical religion (Ps. 78:7).[4]

The Psalm he references is Psalm 78:

> Give ear, O my people, to my teaching;
> incline your ears to the words of my mouth!
> I will open my mouth in a parable;
> I will utter dark sayings from of old, things that we have
> heard and known,
> that our fathers have told us.
> *We will not hide them from their children,*

---

3. MacClaren, *Ibid.*

4. MacClaren, *Ibid.*

but tell to the coming generation
the glorious deeds of the LORD, and his might,
and the wonders that he has done.
He established a testimony in Jacob
and appointed a law in Israel,
which he commanded our fathers
to teach to their children,
that the next generation might know them,
the children yet unborn,
and arise and tell them to their children,
so that they should set their hope in God
and not forget the works of God,
but keep his commandments (Ps. 78: 1-7, emphasis added).

And we are reminded in Psalm 103:

Bless the LORD, O my soul,
and all that is within me,
bless his holy name!
Bless the LORD, O my soul,
and forget not all his benefits,
who forgives all your iniquity,
who heals all your diseases,
who redeems your life from the pit,
who crowns you with steadfast love and mercy,
who satisfies you with good
so that your youth is renewed like the eagle's
(Ps. 103:1-5, emphasis added).

Why memorials? Four reasons:

- **It is quite simple: We forget**. We forget the amazing things God has done in our lives. It's embarrassing, actually. But the fact remains that we get so caught up in the present or are so looking forward to the future that we fail to remember what God has already done.
- **We need them in our dry times**. We need them when we are in the valley. When despair and depressions and disillusionment threaten to overtake us. When doubt and sorrow and suffering block our view of God, we

need to look back and remember Who He is and what He has done.

- **We need them to celebrate God's grace and promises fulfilled**. God's love and grace abound. Memorials act as the spark and tinder for our hearts to burn brightly with love and gratitude to Him.
- **We need them to tell our children and grandchildren about the great things God has done for us**. I look forward to the day my grandchildren ask me, 'Pop Pop, what is that picture?' For who better to tell our children about God's great love than us?

EVEN MEMORIALS DISAPPEAR

Here's a sobering reminder: no worldly memorials exist forever. The fact is that no one will remember any of our own monuments 50 years from now or 100 years from now.

At the beginning of this chapter, I mentioned several items that reminded me of significant moments or accomplishments. And yet:

The IRS Commissioner's Award—No one but me really remembers anything about this award. It was given to me in the early 1990s. I daresay all of the people involved in giving me this award have long forgotten me and the reason for the award.

My marathon medals? They are stored away in a memory chest. Even I rarely look at them. When I die, my children might save them. Or might not. But they won't remember the 26.2 miles that I had to run to get each medal. My runs are already forgotten.

My father's Air Force medals? Neither my brother nor I know what the medals were for. There is no record that we have and no one remains to tell the story. And when he and I are gone, the story will grow dimmer.

All memorials fade. Think of all the great temples and monuments that were erected by previous civilizations. Most of them are gone and the remaining few will go the same way, into oblivion.

Not even the cross remains. For all the brisk business of the relics industry in the early years of Christianity, we do not have the cross that Jesus was crucified on. It's gone. And that's actually a good thing. In heaven, there is a throne, not a cross. We won't celebrate the cross so much as the resurrection. And the throne far better represents that.

These memorials that we set up to honor the Lord's grace in our lifetime? No one will remember them except you and me and a few others. And God. He remembers. He remembers what we celebrated in this life. And whether we celebrated ourselves or His grace.

GOD'S MEMORIAL

There is one more memorial, however, that we should consider. But it isn't one of ours. It is the Lord's.

He has His own memorial:

Behold, I have engraved you on the palms of my hands (Isa. 49:16).

Here is the most precious of memorials. We are engraved on the palms of the Lord. Clearly metaphorical, yet it speaks of the token that is always with the Lord. We are never forgotten. We are always loved. We are always with Him. Each of us. What a glorious image and truth.

Let me conclude with our friend, Mr. Spurgeon on this passage:

'I have engraved you not in the book of record, but I have engraved you upon Myself, upon the palms of My hands.' It means this—I will put it in one short, compact sentence— that Christ could as soon forget Himself as He could forget His people! He has stamped them into Himself! Yes, more—He has taken them into such vital, indelible union with His own person, that to forget one soul that He has bought with blood would be to forget Himself!

Oh, my dear young friends, whose pale faces often grieve me when I see you sad, let us look up to God for comfort! Though you are marked for death, He does not forget you! He will cheer those days of growing weakness, and as you get nearer to the grave, you will also get nearer to heaven! Many a poor woman lying in a lone cottage, or dying in a workhouse, has had more joy than some of the princes of earth in all their wealth and pride. Christ never leaves those who are His in the world, but to them He reveals Himself more sweetly than to others! I would like to say to every child of God here, because God remembers you, all that you lose between here and heaven, He will be sure to give you. All you ask for that is right, you shall have, and a great deal you never thought of asking for! You shall have as much sweet and as much bitter. You shall have as much of everything that is good for you, as shall be best, and afterwards you shall have the fullness, you shall have the glory, for, being engraved on the palms of God's hands, He will not forget to bring you home to the place where He is and to appoint you a mansion among His chosen![5]

The Lord never forgets us. Let that sink in. Even if we forget, He doesn't. What a precious truth.

CONCLUSION

As I wrote this book, two people my age committed suicide: Anthony Bourdain and Kate Spade. One a famous, successful, celebrated chef. The other a well-known and very successful American fashion designer. These were not people deep in old age who died from some terrible disease

---

5. Charles Spurgeon, *God's Memorial of His People*, Sermon published posthumously on January 14, 1915, https://www.spurgeongems.org/vols61-63/chs3441.pdf .

or heart attack. They had lived rich, creative, successful lives and showed no signs of being past their prime. Part of the shock was they were roughly my age. One was two years younger than me, the other two years older. We don't really know why they chose to end their lives. And, sadly, we will continue to see such tragic events with people our age and younger taking their lives.

At a certain time in our lives, it becomes tempting to think that the best is over, that there is no reason to keep going. As tragic as these deaths are, our monuments remind us that we are on a different path. They remind us that we aren't done. They remind us of a God who has been and will be faithful to us. They remind us that how we finish is to be centered in living for Him, glorifying Him.

Here's the final question for you. What have you forgotten that is significant enough that there should be a monument or token or something that will cause you to remember? For we can recall many monuments of grace in our lives. And they all lift up our gaze towards our great and holy and loving God.

For those of us who are closer to the end of our lives, consider the value of such memorials. Being able to see a memorial of some sort and remember the Lord's great love, His provision, His grace, His forgiveness—those are rich, rich reminders. They will help to keep us on the road to finishing well. They will help to adjust our course so we aren't drifting away in sin or in simple aimlessness.

So let us consider how we can better remember Him here. Sin less as we end the race. Have greater faith as the end comes upon us. Celebrate Him better here in preparation for celebrating Him passionately there.

9

Hearts in Heaven

Tis a thing of great consequence to men that their hearts should be in heaven. Men's hearts imply four things: that their thoughts, their choices, their affections and their dependence is there. (Jonathan Edwards)

AUTHOR'S NOTE

Until now, each chapter of this book used the life of someone from long ago as the springboard for the chapter's topic. The nature of this chapter precludes that approach. The reason is that we have no story of a person whose life includes going to heaven and coming back in such sufficient detail that we can wrap a chapter around them. For example, Lazarus died and was brought back to life by Jesus but he gives no report of heaven and we hear nothing more about his life. Likewise, Paul indicates that he was caught up to Paradise (2 Cor. 12: 2-4) but then he tells us that what he heard there he may not tell us. And of course there is the Apostle John, the author of Revelation. He has a vision of heaven but it comes at the end of his life and we have no biblical record of his life afterwards. Did heaven dramatically affect each of them? Of course. But for the purposes of this book, this chapter is an exception to the previous chapters in that we write about heaven without a central character. It is my fervent hope that it still serves you well and provokes you to a greater passion for heaven.

INTRODUCTION

When our children were small, we would go to Cape May, New Jersey, for a week at the beach. Later in life, my wife and I have gone on several cruises with some of our children and their friends. We've traveled to the Caribbean islands and all along the coast of the Mediterranean. We've even cruised to Alaska. Whether with children or grownups, there is always the anticipation of going. We talk about where we are going—the sites we will see, the new vistas, the history, the food, the adventures. We talk about what to expect, to see, and do. Maybe we even save up for a more costly trip. We buy clothes for the adventure. We plan it out. We talk to others who have gone there. We read in preparation for our trip.

I would wager that very few of us do that with heaven, which is quite odd, when you think of it. It says something about us, and not something good, that the most prosperous, highly educated Christians in history think so infrequently about their eternal home. I would argue that finishing well necessarily includes an expectant, joyful, and robust anticipation of heaven. The excitement we have in going on an adventure or vacation is how it should be with heaven. Only more so. Because heaven isn't a vacation. It is our home for eternity.

WHAT ARE WE LOOKING FORWARD TO?

Jonathan Edwards is famous for his sermon about sinners in the hands of an angry God. But listen to this quote about Edwards and heaven and hell:

Edwards did know his hell, but he knew his heaven even better. Anyone who could say that he spoke little of heaven would have amused the people of Northampton who heard hundreds of sermons referring to this celestial theme, many of them exclusively.[1]

Stop and think about this. Edwards' church heard hundreds of sermons that referenced heaven. Hundreds! How many have you heard? In my own experience over forty years, I would venture that I have heard maybe a dozen at most. Certainly not hundreds. In the rich diet of excellent preaching that we can avail ourselves of in today's evangelical church, it is still a rarity to find heart- and mind-inspiring teachings on heaven.

Edwards understood a great truth about the best of Christians:

Tis a thing of great consequence to men that their hearts should be in heaven.[2]

Christian leaders through the ages have taught on heaven and encouraged being heavenly-minded:

Christ brings the heart to heaven first and then the person.[3]

We long for heaven because we long to be nearer God our Father.[4]

To think often and richly about heaven doesn't just get you ready. It reshapes how you live in this life. Death is mitigated. Living is reframed. Eternal truths invade temporal decisions. Even daily choices can be reshaped.

---

1. John Gerstner, *Jonathan Edwards on Heaven and Hell* (Soli Deo Gloria Publications, 1998) p. 9.

2. Gerstner, *Ibid*, p. 9.

3. Richard Baxter, quoted in *The Glory of Christ*.

4. Peter Lewis, *The Glory of Christ*.

And as you travel to the end of this life, thinking about heaven becomes even more compelling.

This chapter is not an exhaustive exploration about heaven but it will, I hope, whet your appetite and provoke your own journey on how you can think about heaven. There are plenty of books already written on the topic that treat this far better than I could hope to here. One book that gripped me many years ago was Randy Alcorn's *Heaven*.[5] You may or may not agree with all he says but, for me, it made me rethink heaven almost completely. I had grown up as a Christian Scientist in which heaven wasn't even the classic caricature of singing angels and saints with halos worshipping forever. Instead, everything was spirit. We were these ever-evolving spiritual entities and God was not in human form. I needed a lot of rethinking from this model. However, even if you are an evangelical Christian, it is likely that your notions of heaven are just that—notions. Writers like Alcorn undo the permission we give ourselves not to think biblically about our eternal home, heaven.

THE BIBLE AND HEAVEN

One of the challenges in thinking about heaven is figuring out what the Bible tells us about heaven. The natural inclination is to look to the book of Revelation. There is plenty of apocalyptic imagery. For example, Revelation 21 describes the New Jerusalem.

> Then I saw a new heaven and a new earth, for the first heaven and the first earth had passed away, and the sea was no more. And I saw the holy city, new Jerusalem, coming down out of heaven from God, prepared as a bride adorned for her husband.
>
> And I heard a loud voice from the throne saying, 'Behold, the dwelling place of God is with man. He will dwell with them, and they will be his people, and

---

5. Randy Alcorn, *Heaven* (Tyndale House Publishers 2004).

God himself will be with them as their God. He will wipe away every tear from their eyes, and death shall be no more, neither shall there be mourning, nor crying, nor pain anymore, for the former things have passed away.'

. . .

The wall was built of jasper, while the city was pure gold, like clear glass. The foundations of the wall of the city were adorned with every kind of jewel. The first was jasper, the second sapphire, the third agate, the fourth emerald, the fifth onyx, the sixth carnelian, the seventh chrysolite, the eighth beryl, the ninth topaz, the tenth chrysoprase, the eleventh jacinth, the twelfth amethyst. And the twelve gates were twelve pearls, each of the gates made of a single pearl, and the street of the city was pure gold, like transparent glass.

. . .

And the city has no need of sun or moon to shine on it, for the glory of God gives it light, and its lamp is the Lamb. By its light will the nations walk, and the kings of the earth will bring their glory into it, and its gates will never be shut by day—and there will be no night there (Rev. 21:1-25).

Revelation has other scenes as well but many people find these scenes unhelpful. We aren't trained to understand apocalyptic literature. Some of it is too fantastical to help us answer the question, 'What is heaven like?' So let me make what may be a surprising suggestion: If you want to know what heaven will be like, don't start with Revelation; rather, start with Genesis.

The Garden of Eden is a much more helpful picture to see what life in heaven will be like. Remember, Eden is the original design for the world. More than that, it suggests the original plan for how God and man would dwell together. Let's reread its description, only this time trying to think of what heaven might be like.

> And the Lord God planted a garden in Eden, in the east, and there he put the man whom he had formed. And out of the ground the Lord God made to spring up every tree that is pleasant to the sight and good for food. The tree of life was in the midst of the garden, and the tree of the knowledge of good and evil. ... The Lord God took the man and put him in the Garden of Eden to work it and keep it. ... Then the Lord God said, 'It is not good that the man should be alone; I will make him a helper fit for him.'
>
> ...
>
> The man gave names to all livestock and to the birds of the heavens and to every beast of the field. But for Adam there was not found a helper fit for him. So the Lord God caused a deep sleep to fall upon the man, and while he slept took one of his ribs and closed up its place with flesh. And the rib that the Lord God had taken from the man he made into a woman and brought her to the man. Then the man said, 'This at last is bone of my bones and flesh of my flesh; she shall be called Woman, because she was taken out of Man.' Therefore a man shall leave his father and his mother and hold fast to his wife, and they shall become one flesh. And the man and his wife were both naked and were not ashamed (Gen. 2:8-25).

I am not suggesting that heaven will be a repeat of Eden, that there will be another garden. But here are several key points that help us get started.

- Eden, and, by extension, heaven, is a place where God and man dwell together. Revelation makes this clear also but Eden presents a more natural and personal picture. We see this in Genesis 3 when God is described as walking in the cool of the day. And Adam and Eve dwelled there naked, without shame.

- Eden, and, by extension, heaven, is a place where man is meant to be engaged in creative and fulfilling vocation. He was to care for the garden. Just as God is the Creator of the heavens and the earth, he was to use our God-given skills and abilities. Many of us aren't sure what we will be doing other than worshipping God. This chapter makes the argument that there is actually much to do.

- Eden, and, by extension, heaven, is perfectly good. Again, Revelation also makes this point but Eden emphasizes it in the sense of how it is to be enjoyed. There is a sense of shalom and harmony between man, creature, and creation. This is a place of great enjoyment.

- Eden, and, by extension, heaven, is a place of perfect relationship with one another. Adam is not meant to be alone. In Eden, Adam has Eve. In heaven, this is extended to an entire people. We aren't alone and we aren't ashamed.

There are important considerations that flow from these observations.

THE NATURE OF HEAVEN

To give us an idea of how to think about heaven, here are three truths to get you started on heaven.

A place of unimaginable and eternal happiness

The pursuit of happiness is one of those emotions that is wired into every person's DNA. You don't have to be a Christian to know that. From the oldest times, happiness has been one of the great treasures of mankind. The Founding Fathers of the United States even enshrined it in the Declaration of Independence, stating, 'We hold these truths to be self-evident, that all men are created equal, that they are endowed by their Creator with certain unalienable Rights that among these are Life, Liberty and the *pursuit of Happiness*.' (Emphasis added.)

The Bible itself makes happiness a key gift of grace. The word 'blessed' simply means happy! When you say that, 'Blessed is the man or woman ...' you are simply saying, 'Happy is the man or woman ...'

What we all know, however, is that happiness is fleeting and impermanent in this world. As much as we try to avoid it, suffering finds us out. And we simply have to read the news to see almost unimaginable pain and tragedy and death around the world. For all the happiness we may be fortunate to have in our life, it is always constrained by the sure reality of suffering in as many forms as there are people, whether by sickness, injury, depression, jealousy, gossip, slander, defeat, betrayal, and, ultimately, death.

Certainly, we can enjoy happiness in this world, not as an end in itself but as it comes from God's grace. But heaven...heaven is a place of unimaginable, continual happiness. How do we know? Revelation 21:4:

> He will wipe away every tear from their eyes, and death shall be no more, neither shall there be mourning, nor crying, nor pain anymore, for the former things have passed away.

How can this be? First, all the causes of unhappiness are removed. All sin and curses are eliminated. The negatives that prevent happiness are gone. Shame? Gone. Anger? Gone. Jealousy? Gone. Fear? Gone. Need? Gone. Secondly, and more importantly, the sources for happiness are eternally present, the most prominent being God Himself.

Of course, because so little is said of heaven, there are plenty of skeptics about such happiness. Bernard Shaw, the famous playwright and atheist, said, 'Heaven, as conventionally conceived, is a place so inane, so dull, so useless, so miserable, that nobody has ever ventured to describe a whole day in heaven, though plenty of people have described a day at the seaside."[6] But this conventional notion of heaven is not the heaven of the Bible.

Consider just one way that the happiness of heaven is experienced: the fellowship of the saints. We shall be together in perfect happiness. There will be great delight in and enjoyment of one another. Consider:

- Friends will be reunited in better relationship than ever was experienced here. Who has gone ahead of you that you are looking forward to seeing again? Maybe it was someone who suffered before dying. I am looking forward to seeing Marva March again. Joe DiBeradino. Sandy Jochum. That won't be dull or useless or miserable. We will see family and friends. What a joyful reunion that will be.

- We won't just be reunited with the closest of friends, but also with people who simply crossed our path in this lifetime. There are dozens and dozens and dozens of acquaintances from church and work and life that I will see again. Only this time, we will have deeper bonds, better reasons to be neighbors in the best of ways.

- Perhaps there were people you knew at church or elsewhere who were estranged from you for some reason. Sins. Offenses. Jealousies. Misunderstandings. Disagreements. Factions. Who don't you speak to anymore but will see in heaven? All past bitterness and offense will be removed. Imagine friendships that are no longer fettered by sinful actions or thoughts. In heaven, you are reconciled. Friendships will be renewed in heaven.

---

6. George Bernard Shaw, *The Collected Plays of George Bernard Shaw – 60 Titles in One Edition* (Musaicum Books, 2017).

- You will meet people in heaven whose presence will surprise you. People you knew but never thought would be there. Maybe they accepted Christ late in life. Maybe they barely made it in. But there they are. And won't that be a wonderful thing to hear their story?
- And more than that, you will be with believers from other times and ages. It will be a happy experience having fellowship with them. People love stories. Imagine hearing about the faith of someone who heard Jesus preach. Or saw His miracles. Or saw Him after He had risen from the dead. Imagine talking to those in the early church. The early martyrs. Imagine talking to the Jews of the Old Testament—Moses, Caleb, Joshua, David. And the countless millions through Old Testament history. We will be able to sit and hear their stories. And then, we hear the stories of those who were saved listening to Calvin. Or who lived in the Middle Ages. Or who were martyred for the faith. Or who have been in heaven for centuries already and can tell you about it.

Think more about this. There will be no mistrust of strangers. No guarded moments. Think of how you must watch out when you are out and about in public. Or how you have to lock your home. No more in heaven. Oh, of course it will be a place of amazing happiness.

Edwards elaborates:

> Heaven is the place of unmixed and unending happiness as incapable of exaggeration as are the miseries of the damned. ... It is sweet here but perfect there; anticipation here, fulfillment there.[7]

And that is just the people.

---

7. Gerstner, *Ibid*, pp. 11-13.

A place of satisfying vocation and activity

I have a very good friend who has worked as an engineer for over thirty years for the same company. For most of that time, the work was not enjoyable. Either he worked for bosses who made the job miserable or the assignments themselves were frustrating. But he had a family to support. So he kept at it faithfully. Thirty years. Work, for many stretches of time, was not pleasant, not enjoyable, not rewarding.

Maybe your experience with work isn't that frustrating but you can identify with the idea that work is something to be endured. Or it is something that you have to do rather than want to do.

That's not the way work was meant by God in the beginning. From the beginning, men and women were created for happy, satisfying work. Adam and Eve worked in the Garden of Eden. They weren't sitting by aimlessly. They had gifts and talents associated with their work. It wasn't until the Fall that the curse of weary work was introduced.

Let me suggest something that the Scriptures hint at: there will be work to do in the New Earth after the consummation of all things. Now before you decide you don't want to go to heaven because of this, consider the following. All of us have certain natural abilities and talents. There are activities and endeavors and work that we like to do and are good at. Some of you are good at engineering. Some of you are artistic. Some of you are great at math. Some of you love to build things. Some of you are writers. Some of you love technology. See where this is going? I simply believe that these talents and abilities cross over with us to heaven. If you like to build things here, how much more would your talents be useful to build things in heaven? If you love art or music, how much more useful is that composing music and creating art in heaven?

If you love math, how much more useful to design things in heaven for the builders to build? What talents do you have? What are you good at? Consider that they are simply preparing you for work in heaven.

I think this is hinted at in the Bible. God Himself made men and women filled with talents to be used for His purposes. Adam and Eve are obvious. But consider what God says in Exodus 35 about those chosen to build the tabernacle:

> Then Moses said to the people of Israel, 'See, the LORD has called by name Bezalel the son of Uri, son of Hur, of the tribe of Judah; and he has filled him with the Spirit of God, *with skill, with intelligence, with knowledge, and with all craftsmanship,* to devise artistic designs, to work in gold and silver and bronze, in cutting stones for setting, and in carving wood, for work in every skilled craft. And he has inspired him to teach, both him and Oholiab the son of Ahisamach of the tribe of Dan. He has filled them with skill to do every sort of work done by an engraver or by a designer or by an embroiderer in blue and purple and scarlet yarns and fine twined linen, or by a weaver—by any sort of workman or skilled designer' (Exod. 35:30-35, emphasis added).

In heaven, we all will be filled with the Holy Spirit. And all of us will be useful to God. Do you feel your work here on earth is useless? It won't be in heaven. You will be filled with skill to do what God wants done in the new heaven and the new earth.

Whereas work in this life is tinged by the Fall, all work in heaven will be satisfying and joyful. It will be a happy thing to work. No weariness of the soul. No sense of pointless toil. No strain of fear or terror of failure. Work won't be work as we know it here. It will simply be what we like to do.

Have you ever worked at something, finished it, and been really happy with the results? Have you had friends who did a really good job at work and told you excitedly about it? Work will make us happy and satisfied.

A locality, a place, completely enlivened by the presence of God

And here is the most important truth about heaven: God is there.

Oh yes, He is everywhere equally present in the universe. But heaven is a place, a fixed place. And it is there that His presence is particularly manifested. Revelation says His glory is such that there will be no need for a sun to light heaven. And more than that? Jesus, the Son of God, is physically present there. The God/Man. The risen Savior and King. He will be there. You and I will see Him face to face.

What makes heaven heaven? God is there. God makes heaven heaven.

Too much is made of the description of heaven to the devaluation of why heaven is so special. Does it really matter whether there are real roads of gold? Does it really matter if there are physical walls of precious gems? What matters is that the living God dwells there among His people.

If you have been to certain places, they are special because of the beauty of nature. To this day, I can remember seeing the Grand Canyon for the first time. I was twelve years old and went there with my parents. And when I went to the rim, I felt things I had never felt before. It was an inexpressible sense of awe. I felt as if something inside of me had been born. It was as if I were connected to something greater than myself.

I've felt similar things elsewhere to a lesser degree: the Bavarian countryside, the rice fields of India, the moonscape in northern India, the brilliant blue waters of the Caribbean, the sweeping panorama of the Alps.

Other places are special because of their manmade grandeur or wealth or awesomeness. How amazing to see the pyramids or Versailles or the Sears Tower or the monastery of Montserrat.

Even your home has a special quality. It is the place where your life is centered. Comfortable. Yours. Not a strange place.

Heaven is all of these and more. It is enlivened by the presence of God. Gerstner quotes Edwards:

> The external heaven surrounds Christ not merely as a house surrounds an inhabitant or a palace surrounds a prince or as stones and timber encompass a land. But rather as plants and flowers are before the sun that have their life and beauty and being from that luminary or as the sun may be encompassed around with reflections of his brightness as the cloud of glory in Mount Sinai surrounded Christ there.[8]

Heaven itself is 'alive in Christ.' Unlike any other place. Completely and unimaginably more wonderful than any place.

And here is a final thought about God in heaven. We will be continually discovering more about God for all eternity. The greatness and glory of God is boundless. Think of listening to a great symphony and thinking you've heard the best only to hear a new symphony that is even better. Think of tasting the most wonderful food only to discover there is even better tasting food. God will be like that. The eternal God, the sovereign God, the holy God, the God of love—we will never exhaust ourselves in learning about Him. And doesn't that make sense based on our nature? We are created to be learners, ever learning. We have the faculties of curiosity and growing intelligence. In heaven, we will meet the perfect subject of that nature—the eternal, glorious Creator of the universe Himself, who can never be

---

8. Gerstner, *Ibid*, p. 16.

fully known but who delights in revealing Himself to His people. What a glorious place heaven will be.

Moving Our Hearts To Heaven

How does this help us finish well? Jonathan Edwards explains:

> Tis a thing of great consequence to men that their hearts should be in heaven. Men's hearts imply four things: that their thoughts, their choices, their affections and their dependence is there.[9] (Emphasis added.)

When your heart moves more from this life to heaven, it changes everything you do and are in this life. Where do your thoughts emanate from? Do you make choices with heaven in mind? Are your affections, your feelings, grounded in this world only? Are you dependent on the treasure of this world or the security of being in heaven?

When heaven invades this earth and our hearts, we cannot but change how we live. It doesn't have to be seismic changes. But we make sacrifices, make plans on where to live, even choose lines of work and vocation with heaven in mind. Our grip on worldly pleasures is loosened. What the world values, we don't value as much or at all.

Admittedly, all of us tend to be too wrapped up in this world. How do we move our hearts towards heaven more? Certainly traumatic natural events can make us think of heaven:

- Death of a friend or family member
- Serious sickness
- Rough change in life circumstances (loss of job, divorce)

And simply getting older also makes us start to think more of it. Our own approaching death forces our attention heavenward.

9. Gerstner, *Ibid*, p. 9.

But there is a better way. There is no reason not to start now thinking more about heaven and thinking about how our choices on how we live and who we are prepare us for heaven here in this life. Here are just a few ways to be proactive in moving our hearts towards heaven:

- **Pursue holiness intentionally.**
This may sound odd. We are called to be holy as God is holy. But getting rid of sin and putting on righteousness aims us towards heaven because it removes the veil of this world so we can look ahead and see what our eternal life will be like.

  Sin roots us in this life. The love of sin, the love of our flesh, blocks our view of heaven, distracts us from thinking about heaven.

  Putting off sin and pursuing a life of holiness not only removes the wall between us and heaven but helps us want heaven more. The more we taste God's holiness, the more we realize that we are not made to be permanent citizens here in this life.

  And a special encouragement and caution to older readers: pursuing holiness might just be more important the older you get. There is a temptation I've experienced of wanting to give up fighting against sinful behavior the older I get. Soldiers get weary in battle. So do aging Christians. If Caleb kept fighting his enemies at eighty-five, let's not grow weary in the battle against the sin in our lives.

- **Read about heaven.**
If you are like me, I need to read about something to get started thinking about it more. So it is with heaven. Start with the Scriptures. Do a Bible study on heaven. Read great books about heaven. Challenge your cultural notions about heaven and replace them with a rich, biblical understanding of heaven.

The closer I get to a special trip or vacation, the more excited I get because I have ideas and plans and things I want to do. Why shouldn't it be the same as we finish the race? Learn more, study more, get ready because it isn't a dream vacation; it is better and forever.

I've mentioned Randy Alcorn. But if you want a richer diet, read the Puritans. They will challenge you to think far more than you have now about heaven.

- **Think about heaven.**
  What do you daydream about? Maybe retirement? Maybe time with your family? Maybe getting married? Maybe the next vacation? Maybe buying a house?

  Let me suggest that you begin to daydream and meditate on heaven. Christian meditation isn't about clearing your mind of all thoughts. It's about focusing on a single thing and turning it around in your mind. You can do that with a passage of Scripture. And you can do it about heaven.

  Because when you come out of such meditation, you come out with a fresh mindset about what you've been thinking about. If you've been daydreaming about a vacation, you come out of that reverie and think to yourself, 'Darn it! I am going to do it!'

  The same with heaven. Think great thoughts about heaven. I've suggested that there will be soul-satisfying work in heaven. Do you agree?
  o   What work might you do in heaven if that is true?
  o   What kind of enjoyments might there be? Sports? Arts? Concerts? Plays?
  o   Paul writes about our resurrection bodies in heaven. What will they be like?
  o   Will we have bodies in heaven when we die (before Jesus comes again)?
  o   Will we live in houses? Condos?

- o How do I get to speak to Moses? Abraham? Paul? Is there a sign-up sheet?
- o Who would I want to see most, other than Jesus?
- o What will the government look like (besides Jesus being king)?
- o Will there be schools?
- o There is no marriage in heaven. How does that work?
- o How will we travel in heaven?
- o There is no sea but are there rivers and lakes? Can we go swimming?
- o What will we eat? Will there be great cooks? Do we cook our own food? Where will we eat?
- o Will there be animals? There were in Eden, why not heaven?
- o Will we see our pets?
- o And most of all, what will it be like to be with Jesus? Will we walk with Him like Adam did in the Garden of Eden? What would you talk about? What will you want to know?

When you come out of those sweet thoughts, think about how to live your life here. And how to get there well.

CONCLUSION

Let me finish with Mr. Burroughs who says it far better than I could:

> If the Lord should rip open our hearts and show them to all the world, I hope the world would see that heaven is stamped on our hearts. We count it sad weather when we cannot see the heavens for many days, when we cannot see heaven many times, for a week.
>
> We consider it a bad home where men dwell in narrow lanes in the city, so that they can barely see the heavens unless they go into the fields. My brethren, surely it is a sad

time with a gracious heart when one day passes without conversing with heaven, without the sight of heaven, without meditations of heaven, without having hearts there. Thus it should be Christians whose conversations are in heaven. They should never love such buildings wherein they cannot see the beams of heaven. It is a most comfortable thing to see the light. To a man that dwells in some dark house, it is very comforting to walk out in the open air and behold the heavens. Oh my brethren! Our souls dwell in dark houses, every one of us, for our bodies are to our souls like a dark and low cellar, but the Lord gives us the liberty to go abroad, to be conversing with the things of heaven that He has revealed in His Word and in His ordinances.

Many citizens that live in dark rooms and work long hours, on days of recreation take long walks in the fields and smell the fresh air. How delightful it is to them. The same should be true of a gracious heart, even though he has much business in the world.[10]

Consider: If you are reading this, you most likely will be dead in 100 years. If you are saved in Christ, you will be in heaven. After 10,000 years, you will still be there. One million years. This lifetime, this blink of an eye, in eternity it will seem awfully small. Live well here. But live life knowing that the best is yet to come. Get ready for it.

With whatever time we have left in this life, let's live with heaven actively in mind. Let's have heaven stamped on our heart. And let's do so to the glory of God until that day when we arrive.

---

10. Jeremiah Burroughs, *A Treatise of Earthly-Mindedness* (Soli Deo Gloria Publications, 1991), p. 99.

Conclusion

Better is the end of a thing than its beginning. (Eccles. 7:8)

A few concluding remarks.

THE ENTIRE GAME MATTERS BUT THE FINISH ...

It's interesting that the end of a sports event is often better remembered than the beginning of the event. Everyone in our family is an Alabama football fan thanks to my wife who was born at the university hospital in Tuscaloosa. We all can still recount in great detail the winning touchdown in the 2017 Championship game against Georgia. It was the last play of the game in overtime and 'Bama won on a long pass after taking a long loss the previous play. Roll Tide! But I have no memory of the kickoff or the second play of the game. Or the third. If you like sports, it's probably the same for your team. You remember that last big play or simply the game ending. It's ironic because every minute of the game mattered. A team cannot not play for the first 59 minutes of a 60 minute game and then play real hard in the last minute and expect to win. But it's often the end that we remember. I think that is true, not just because of the last big play but because of the outcome. Alabama won! Yay! Clemson won the year before! Boo!

Life is like that. We have to 'play' the entire game. What we do at 25 is just as important as what we do at 65. But the outcome is often what is most remembered. We all finish. But how did we finish? Caleb finished well. Solomon, Lot and Demas did not. Hence, Ecclesiastes 7:8 says, 'Better is the end of a thing than its beginning.' We get lots of chances to get it right throughout our life but it's the end that tells the story in a special way.

FINISHING BADLY DOESN'T MEAN NOT BEING SAVED

Throughout the book, we've looked at this idea of finishing well. I want to make clear again that we aren't making the case that everyone who finishes badly is unsaved. I think we will see Solomon in heaven. And Lot. Maybe even Demas. We will see David, whose finish in no way could be termed good. And Samson? Likely. The point of this book was not to say that finishing bad puts you outside heaven when you die; rather, how you finish is a matter of your relationship with your Savior and that will matter so much more when you die.

HOW DOES THIS HELP WITH REAL LIFE?

As Americans, we are an action-focused society. Need to lose weight? Tell me what to do. Need to succeed at business? Tell me what to do. How do I raise my children? How do I have a good marriage? Tell me what to do.

This book did not answer those life questions. On purpose. Underlying all of these very important questions is the idea that our core, our greatest treasure, will drive how we live our life. If Jesus is your treasure, you will live life a certain way. You will love your spouse a certain way. You will raise your children a certain way. Before you ask the important question, 'What should I do?', get to the core of who you are and what your treasures are. Then ask the questions of how to put it into practice.

PAUL'S FINAL WORDS

Paul stands out as our last biblical teacher on finishing well. The last letter he wrote was 2 Timothy. It is a somber letter, for Paul has been arrested by the Romans a second time and it is clear to him that he won't be released this time. His death is fast approaching. Paul, in chains, in prison, is facing execution. It is a sobering reflection. He is confined. By Roman law, he is possibly chained to a Roman soldier. What support he gets comes from a few friends. Others have deserted him. This great man of God is reduced to such a state. And what are some of his final written words?

> For I am already being poured out as a drink offering, and the time of my departure has come. I have fought the good fight, I have finished the race, I have kept the faith. Henceforth there is laid up for me the crown of righteousness, which the Lord, the righteous judge, will award to me on that day, and not only to me but also to all who have loved his appearing (2 Tim. 4:6-8).

Those are not the words of a man finishing poorly. In spite of the ignoble condition in which his life is ending, Paul's view is not on his circumstances. He is looking somewhere else. He acknowledges he is about to die. He will be poured out. The race is finished. But he is looking ahead and upward. He has kept the faith. He awaits that moment when he will see his Savior again. Face to face.

I hope my final words are like that. When I finish this race it won't be that Marine at the end of the Marine Corps Marathon congratulating me at the finish line. My great hope and desire is that it will be the Son of God, the wonderful Savior I love. Face to face. What will He say? Oh, how I hope it is, 'Well done, good and faithful servant. Come and share your master's happiness.' I don't know how it will turn out yet. The race isn't over. I am still making choices. I am still fighting the fight. Still working on that great treasure.

ON THE DAY YOU DIE

On the day you breathe your last, you will meet Him face to face. On that day all you will take with you is your life story. No one goes with you. You take nothing of this world. Hopefully, you will be met by a loving Savior who will welcome you into your eternal dwelling place. And in that sacred and intimate moment, both you and He will know how you lived and how you finished. Nothing will be hidden from Him. Every action, every word, every thought will be known between the two of you. And as much as He loves you, if you finished poorly, you will have to look into His eyes and realize that His grace had to cover much more than it should have.

I don't believe that we will carry guilt into heaven but I do think we will remember our lives here and there will be some kind of heavenly 'regret' about how we lived below the privilege of being saved. Maybe it will be a new kind of emotion. (There's another thought for you about heaven. Will there be new emotions in heaven? There must be for the new experiences we will have there.) Remembering our sins in this life won't condemn us; in fact, it will probably make us love Him and worship Him all the more. But somehow, I think it will also make us go, 'Oh ... I could have done so much better.'

If you finish well, however, consider the day you die. At that moment when you breathe your last, there He will be. And you will see it in His eyes and hear it in His voice,

'Well done, good and faithful servant! Come and share your Master's happiness.' Don't you long for that? God's exuberant, loving, and happy commendation? Wouldn't that make all the sacrifices and faith and self-denial worthwhile? Imagine Jesus turning to the witnesses there, ready to welcome you and hear Him say, 'See this one? He finished well. She finished well. And I am so happy!' The Bible indicates that there are rewards in heaven for what we do in this lifetime but I would trade them all to hear that from Jesus. Wouldn't you?

I look forward to seeing you in heaven and hearing about your finish.

Gone From My Sight

I am standing upon the seashore. A ship, at my side,
spreads her white sails to the moving breeze and
starts
for the blue ocean. She is an object of

beauty and strength.
I stand and watch her until, at length,

she hangs like a speck
of white cloud just where the sea and sky

come to mingle with each other.

Then, someone at my side says, 'There, she is gone.'

Gone where?

Gone from my sight. That is all.

She is just as large in mast,
hull and spar as she was when she left my side.
And, she is just as able to bear her load of living
freight to her destined port.

Her diminished size is in me—not in her.

And, just at the moment when someone says,

'There, she is gone,'
there are other eyes watching her coming,

and other voices
ready to take up the glad shout, 'Here she comes!'

And that is dying ...

(Henry Van Dyke)

Also available from Christian Focus Publications...

STOPPED WORK?

encouraging stories of new directions in retirement

START LIVING!

IRENE HOWAT

Stopped Work? Start Living!

Encouraging stories of directions in new retirement
Irene Howat

Western society is undergoing a transformation. With more and more of us living into our eighties and nineties, elderly and retired people constitute a more significant sector of the population than ever before. For many, retirement is looked upon as an opportunity to take up residence at the golf club, however, for the Christian it can offer so much more!

With a wealth of experience and wisdom many Christians find retirement gives the opportunity to serve God in new and different ways. 'God opens unexpected doors' tells the story of retirees who, having left the workplace behind them, took up the challenge of further Christian service. These inspirational examples show us that whilst others may view retirement as a time to wind down, we as Christians should view it as a new opportunity to serve the Lord Jesus.

ISBN: 978-1-84550-047-4

Christian Focus Publications

Our mission statement —

STAYING FAITHFUL
In dependence upon God we seek to impact the world through literature faithful to His infallible Word, the Bible. Our aim is to ensure that the Lord Jesus Christ is presented as the only hope to obtain forgiveness of sin, live a useful life and look forward to heaven with Him.

Our books are published in four imprints:

CHRISTIAN FOCUS

Popular works including biographies, commentaries, basic doctrine and Christian living.

CHRISTIAN HERITAGE

Books representing some of the best material from the rich heritage of the church.

MENTOR

Books written at a level suitable for Bible College and seminary students, pastors, and other serious readers. The imprint includes commentaries, doctrinal studies, examination of current issues and church history.

CF4•K

Children's books for quality Bible teaching and for all age groups: Sunday school curriculum, puzzle and activity books; personal and family devotional titles, biographies and inspirational stories — because you are never too young to know Jesus!

Christian Focus Publications Ltd,
Geanies House, Fearn, Ross-shire,
IV20 1TW, Scotland, United Kingdom.
www.christianfocus.com
blog.christianfocus.com